The Engines of the Night

Science Fiction Novels

THE EMPTY PEOPLE
THE MEN INSIDE
OVERLAY
IN THE ENCLOSURE
UNDERLAY
UNIVERSE DAY
BEYOND APOLLO
HEROVIT'S WORLD
GUERNICA NIGHT
CONVERSATIONS
THE SODOM AND GOMORRAH
    BUSINESS
THE DESTRUCTION OF THE
    TEMPLE
PHASE IV
THE GAMESMAN
ON A PLANET ALIEN
REVELATIONS
DWELLERS OF THE DEEP
GATHER IN THE HALL OF THE
    PLANETS
THE FALLING ASTRONAUTS
THE DAY OF THE BURNING
TACTICS OF CONQUEST
GALAXIES
SCOP
CHORALE
THE LAST TRANSACTION
PROSE BOWL (with Bill
    Pronzini)
THE CROSS OF FIRE

Collections

FINAL WAR & OTHER
    FANTASIES
IN THE POCKET AND OTHER
    SF STORIES
THE MANY WORLDS OF BARRY
    MALZBERG

OUT FROM GANYMEDE AND
    OTHER SF STORIES
THE BEST OF BARRY N.
    MALZBERG
DOWN HERE IN THE DREAM
    QUARTER
MALZBERG AT LARGE
THE MAN WHO LOVED THE
    MIDNIGHT LADY

Anthologies

FINAL STAGE (with Edward
    L. Ferman)
ARENA (with Edward L.
    Ferman)
GRAVEN IMAGES (with
    Edward L. Ferman)
DARK SINS, DARK DREAMS
    (with Bill Pronzini)
THE END OF SUMMER: SF IN
    THE FIFTIES (with Bill
    Pronzini)
SHARED TOMORROWS (with
    Bill Pronzini)
BUG-EYED MONSTERS (with
    Bill Pronzini)
NEGLECTED VISIONS (with
    Martin Harry Greenberg
    and Joseph D. Olander)
THE ARBOR HOUSE TREASURY
    OF MODERN HORROR FICTION
    (with Bill Pronzini and
    Martin Harry Greenberg)

Nonfiction

THE ENGINES OF THE NIGHT:
    SCIENCE FICTION IN THE
    EIGHTIES

The Engines
of the Night

Science Fiction in the Eighties

BARRY N. MALZBERG

DOUBLEDAY & COMPANY, INC.
GARDEN CITY, NEW YORK
1982

Some of these essays, many in far different form, have
appeared in *Analog, Analog Yearbook, Science Fiction Review,
Empire Science Fiction, Heavy Metal,* and *Amazing Stories.*

Library of Congress Cataloging in Publication Data

Malzberg, Barry N.
The engines of the night.

1. Science fiction—History and criticism—Addresses, ↙
essays, lectures.   I. Title.
PN3433.8.M34   809.3′876
AACR2
ISBN: 0-385-17541-8
Library of Congress Catalog Card Number 81–43148

First Edition

DEDICATION IN MEMORIAM

Mark Clifton
Edmond Hamilton
Cyril M. Kornbluth
Henry Kuttner

Contents

". . . the aggregate amount I paid out as an editor to everybody, over a period of thirty years from 1939 to 1969, as editor of *Astonishing Stories* and *Super Science Stories,* as editor of the *Star* series of original anthologies for Ballantine, as editor of more than a dozen reprint anthologies over that period and finally as editor of *Galaxy, If, Worlds of Tomorrow* and others for nearly a decade—the total of checks, for all of them put together, to every contributor, is probably about [a] quarter of a million."

Frederik Pohl
1979

"Almost everybody in science fiction tends to stay in science fiction."

Henry Morrison
1978

Introduction

These essays were written by a man whose first science fiction story appeared in the late nineteen-sixties, who rose to minor prominence in the early to mid-seventies, watched his career suddenly (and not entirely on his own responsibility) plummet in the middle of the decade, and who spent the last of the seventies lurching toward the Bethlehem of 1980, not so much trying to be born again, as to assess the roughness of the beast. The career in many ways paralleled the arc of political and social consciousness through that period: the questioning of institutions and institutionally propounded insight, the rocking of those institutions, and then, after Nixon's eviction in the middle of the period, a speedy and effective counterrevolution which got some of us out of the temple right quick.

I have not had (I raise my right hand) the most successful or prominent career in science fiction in the seventies but I have had, I think, the most clearly symptomatic—the career which did indeed most survive in reaction to the larger political and social developments of that time. The perspective is peculiarly mine, of course; I make no claims for its universality. If anything, I argue the other way: for its particularity. No one right now could regard science fiction in quite this way.

Any of us who read or write in the field can make that statement, of course. We behold what we have become. But if there is any particular cachet to my perspective it comes because my career is, perhaps more than some, metaphoric.

And then, maybe it is not. My career is no way for a young

science fiction writer; I am no model of a Modern Major General. Reading and writing a lot of science fiction over a long period (and long it has been) will if nothing else grant humility: modestly garbed in sackcloth and cosmeticized with ashes, I sally beyond the mirror at my own risk now and in only a modestly adventurous spirit.

But I *never*, as I kept on reminding myself through the decade, had possessed ambitions which were initially large-scale. Science fiction had not been much more than an experiment. How far could I go . . . what could I get done . . . what could I say . . . how much could I get through, before they caught on or caught up? was the basic question. What would science fiction do—not so much to the world, but to *me?*

I found out.

Surely did.

1980: New Jersey

The Engines of the Night

The Number of the Beast

Well, what *is* it? Fifty experts—as the old Yiddish saying might have it—will produce fifty-one definitions. Still, we all try; here I am in Collier's Encyclopedia:

"Science fiction is that form of literature which deals with the effects of technological change in an imagined future, an alternative present or a reconceived history."

Workable and cautious, but it does not evade what could be called the *Arrowsmith* problem—Sinclair Lewis's novel, that is, which all of us science-fictioneers would instinctively agree is *not* of the genre, would probably fall into it under the terms of this definition. Certainly, technological (medical) change is an important aspect of this novel as are the effects of science upon the protagonist and his marriage. Clearly, my definition would also exclude some of the whimsical short stories of Robert Sheckley, whose bemused characters face the absurdities of a slightly disorienting metaphysics in the recognizable present: there is nothing technological about these stories, much less concern with technological change, and yet they appeared, most of them, in Horace Gold's *Galaxy* and fit indistinguishably into the format of that magazine. On the basis of this kind of work Sheckley was recognized in early career as one of the most promising of the new writers. My definition would also exclude Randall Garrett's Darcy series whose novels and novelette depict an alternate present in which magic has assumed the role of science and modern science never found its way into being discovered. Change, to be sure, but not technological change:

here is genre science fiction that deals with technological absence.

Shrug, consider the bar bill, try Theodore Sturgeon's nineteen-forties dictum: a good science fiction story is one whose events would not have occurred without its scientific content. This is promising—among other things, it manages to summarize, for the decade, the essence of John W. Campbell's editorial vision in *Astounding* . . . but Anne McCaffrey's dragons could not fly in Sturgeon's science fiction and Sheckley's work, right through his great novel *Dimension of Miracles*, would not fit. Nor would the visions of J. G. Ballard and his descendants; if *The Terminal Beach* or *The Drowned World* are about anything, they are about a world in which science has failed and gone away . . . and yet the works of Ballard are considered central to any understanding of post-1960s science fiction.

James Tiptree's famous *The Women Men Don't See* has no science in it either, nor does Robert Silverberg's 1972 novel *Dying Inside*, generally regarded as one of the pivotal works of the decade. (It concerns a telepath, who has lived concealing his gift, slowly losing his powers in early middle age in contemporary New York.) Then, too, Sturgeon's definition would admit not only *Arrowsmith* but many novels *about* science—Morton Thompson's *Not As a Stranger*, Peter George's *Red Alert*, George P. Elliott's *David Knudsen*. Any definition so inclusive would obviously attenuate a category which, however ill-defined, is very clearly understood by its readers, writers, editors and critics to be a distinct and limited (if not really limiting) form of literature.

Perhaps one throws up one's hands and dives back to the fifties to Damon Knight's "Science fiction is whatever we point to when we say 'this is science fiction.'" Lots of truth in that; whatever trouble we may have with definitions, there is a consensual feeling among those of us who pretend to understand the form: McCaffrey's *Dragonflight* belongs in the genre and *Arrowsmith* does not. Check the Science Fiction Encyclopedia and the bibliographies. Still, if Knight's path of implied least resistance is the way to go, I would prefer Frederik Pohl's useful, provocative and contained: "Science fiction is a way of thinking about things."

Science fiction, then, is a methodology and an approach.

Pohl is surely on the trail of something important here, and if one could define what that way of thinking about things *is*, one perhaps would come as close to a working definition of science fiction as will be needed to understand almost all of it. Let me have a try at this, noting my indebtedness to A. J. Budrys, who has prowled this corridor some, most notably in his introduction to John Varley's collection *The Persistence of Vision*.

Science fiction, at the center, holds that the encroachment of technological or social change will make the future different and that it will *feel* different to those within it. In a technologically altered culture, people will regard themselves and their lives in ways that we cannot apprehend. That is the base of the science fiction vision, but the more important part comes as corollary: the effects of a changed technology upon us will be more profound than change brought about by psychological or social pressure. What technological alteration, the gleaming or putrid knife of the future, is going to do will cut far deeper than the effects of adultery, divorce, clinical depression, rap groups, consciousness raising, encounter sessions or even the workings of that famous old law firm of Sack, Pillage, Loot & Burn. It will be *these* changes—those imposed extrinsically by force—which really matter; this is what the science fiction writer is saying, and in their inevitability and power they trivialize the close psychological interactions in which most of us transact our lives (or at least would like to).

Lasting, significant change, science fiction says, is uncontrollable and coming in uncontrollably; regardless of what we think or how we feel, we have lost control of our lives. When the aliens debark from their craft to deal with the colonization assignment, the saved and the unsaved, adulterous and chaste, psychoanalyzed and decompensated will be caught in their terrible tracer beams and absorb the common fate. When the last layer of protective ozone is burned out by International Terror & Trade, discussion leaders, the born again and the members of the American Psychological Association will all go together.

This is what was being said, implicitly, in all of the crazy and convoluted stories of the thirties and forties behind the funny covers; more sedately, and occasionally in hardcover, it is being said today. Because this vision is inimical to the middle class (which has been taught that increased self-realization is increased control), because it tends to trivialize if not actually mock the vision of the modern novel and drama (the shaping of experience is its explanation), genre science fiction has been in trouble in America from the outset. It has been perceived almost from the beginning as the enemy of the culture. Science fiction has had a hearing from those who control access to the broad reading audience at only a few points in its history (I suggest 1946, 1957 and 1972) and in every case has been swiftly repudiated. The successful media science fiction of the seventies (most, though not all of it, debased adventure stories with crude science-fictional props) has forced literary science fiction into juxtaposition with the culture. The increase in readership funneled in by "Star Trek" and *Star Wars* has indicated that publishers will not permit it this time to go away . . . but science fiction is hardly, at the outset of the decade of the eighties, much more of a reputable and critically accepted genre than it was thirty years ago.

It is my assumption that it never will be. Science fiction is too threatening.

At the center, science fiction is a dangerous literature. It represents the beast born in the era of enlightenment to snarl at the heart of all intellectual and technological advance. As the technology becomes more sophisticated and intrusive, as our lives in the postindustrial twentieth came to be dominated in every way by technology, science fiction became more cunning in its template. We know not what we do; the engines can eat us up—this is what science fiction has been saying (among many other things) for a long time now. It may be preaching only to the converted, but the objective truth, the inner beast, will not go away and so neither— despite the hostility of the culture, the ineptitude of many of its practitioners, the loathing of most of its editors, the corruption of most of its readers—neither will science fiction. It, if no given writer, will persist; will run, with the engines, the full disastrous course.

Some notes on how it ran and how it runs follow, at length and in humility.

1980: New Jersey

L'État c'est moi

In mid-1969, as the recently appointed and juvenescent (twenty-nine is not an age, as the poet should have pointed out; it is a condition) editor of the *Bulletin,* the semimonthly publication of the then four-year-old Science Fiction Writers of America (SFWA), I wrote and published an editorial mildly critical of NASA's public relations and of the Apollo project itself. It was written in reminiscence of the December 1968 mission captained by Frank Borman in which the moon was circled and Genesis liberally quoted; the invocation of the Old Testament seemed to me a failure of church/state separation and also an interference with what might have been private responses to a voyage which struck me as over-ridingly significant and mystical. I said all of this in a rather halting fashion (I did not then have much of a handle on the personal essay) and kept it to a decent four hundred words and devoted the remainder of that issue, once again, to market reports, contract summaries and communications amongst SFWA members, most of whom appeared to be not greatly enamored of one another.

Cries of pain and rage descended as if by parachute upon the modest premises in New York where the hapless publication and hapless remarks had been prepared. They descended also upon the quarters of the SFWA officers and trustees and these worthies, conferring shortly thereafter, decided and rapidly informed me that my services in science fiction were more urgently needed elsewhere and right away . . . I should immediately become a full-time writer in this field, that was to say. Would I please? Now? Write only fiction, that was to say. Clearly the officers did not wish the editorship of the *Bulletin* to interfere with my burgeoning career, and I was sent on my way from that volunteer position with due regard and extreme haste. (I thought at the time that to be fired as a volunteer was some kind of low, but learned as the years went on that science fiction offered humiliations more intricate and absolute.)

Why? I hear a question from the back. What's going on? I'm kind of new here; why did they fire you for what you call a few mild anti-NASA, anti-Borman remarks? NASA went down the tubes a long time ago and Borman's working for an airline, isn't he? On television commercials and all that. Everybody knows that Apollo didn't play downtown. You were speaking for the majority. Unless, of course, those remarks *weren't* so mild. You always had a tendency to underestimate your effect on people.

Well, maybe I did. Point conceded. Nonetheless, let me tell this in my own way; it is a shade elliptical but in the end all will come clear, as the widow said to the bishop. My correspondents seemed in the main to think of science fiction as a kind of research and development arm of a technology administered by the government.

To them—and they represented the SFWA at the time and probably now, although the focus of the argument has shifted—the field was not so much to be an arena of exploration and debate (as many of us who came into science fiction in the sixties had been encouraged by the climate of the times and Michael Moorcock to think) as it was Gernsback's Flowering—it existed to popularize technological advance, to dazzle the unsophisticated public with visions of the machinery and miracles to come. That was what Gernsback wanted, all right (with the secondary ambition of interesting young men in science as a career—and however Hugo may have failed in that secondary aim, we now know that he succeeded completely with the first).

Of course I had taken a different view. (I usually do.) I thought at the time that I spoke for many readers and writers. The evolution of the field literarily and stylistically through the thirties and forties and the introduction (almost from the outset of Campbell's editorship) of a strong dystopian element in speculation (which Horace Gold seized and brought to the center of the field) had led me to feel by 1969 that it was late in the day indeed, and that science fiction had a more important role to play in the culture than to serve as a cheerleader for technological advance. I thought that NASA was the public relations arm of the scientific establishment. I thought that both were pimping for Johnson's slut of a war tucked away (so Johnson hoped) in the back district. I thought a lot of things.

I also feel, more than a decade later, that I was right, that my attitude in time prevailed not only in the country but in the field itself; that my attitude was symptomatic of much of the serious work done in the decade . . . but I am also sure that I misjudged the feelings of most of the writers and all of the editors. These people did not regard science fiction so much as a speculative medium as one functional to the prevailing standards of the culture.

There was fear in those letters. One correspondent who worked for the space industry felt that his job was threatened, that he might actually lose it if the *Bulletin* reached his superiors, who would find him the member of an organization whose official voice questioned their practices. (He might have been right.) The fear was less personally based elsewhere but no less palpable: where did I get off knocking NASA and the government, the President and Borman, the church and the Bible for heaven's sake, just when the Apollo project and the enormous attention it garnered were on the verge of making science fiction an acceptable pursuit?

This was a core argument. It was not hard for me to understand it even at the time. For decades, science fiction readers and writers had been regarded by the academic/literary nexus and the media as a bizarre group, aficionados of the subliterate obsessed by the arcane; now Borman and the boys were making all those crazy stories appear somewhat predictive.

Just at the point where a science fiction writer might finally get a hearing at the universities or by a Hollywood agent, an official voice was railing against their great patron. Didn't I—well, didn't I understand how it used to be? Didn't I remember how the magazines went to rout in the fifties and how for decades a science fiction writer could not even be regarded as a *writer* by the most miserable graduate assistant in English?

Didn't I remember how academically connected writers had been forced to publish under pseudonyms in the forties because revelation of their sf orientation to the department head might have threatened their position? Didn't I remember those two-cent-a-word (at the top) magazine rates and $500 all-rights book contracts?

What was wrong with me, anyway? If I had objections to the spirit or public relations of the project, why didn't I put them in my bag of pretensions and where the moon don't shine? Was I out to destroy science fiction? If science fiction appeared in the position of speaking against NASA or Apollo, what man in the street would ever take us seriously again? One correspondent attacked not my arguments but my grammar. Another suggested that I was merely jealous. (I had a few defenders but they came in late and semiapologetic. First Amendment and all that.)

So, tossed out, I went away at least from the *Bulletin* (eventually I went away from the SFWA but that is another, less interesting and symptomatic issue, and sometime later I even came *back* but that is the least interesting of all), but I took from the experience a not unenduring lesson. (Hard spankings are meant to do this, I kindly told my daughter: make you remember.) That lesson has been further articulated in the *Collected Works*—and a good thing too, since we all must write from experience and almost every full-time writer is shorter on it than he would like to admit.

The lesson was this:

Science fiction, for all its trappings, its talk of "new horizons" and "new approaches" and "thinking things through from the beginning" and "new literary excitement," is a very conservative form of literature. It is probably more conservative than westerns, mysteries or gothics, let alone that most reactionary of all literatures, pornography. Most of its writers and editors are genuinely troubled by innovative styles or concepts at the outset, because they have a deep stake by the time they have achieved any position in the field in *not appearing crazy*. This was certainly true in 1969 when the field was still a minor if marginally respectable genre. It is more true yet at the beginning of the eighties when it has become, for a concatenation of factors, perhaps the most predictably profitable part of the publishing subdivisions of many conglomerates and when licensing of "Star Trek" or the Lucas properties is worth hundreds of millions of dollars. The conservative nature of science fiction today is no longer an intimation, not even a standard. It is a necessity.

Very difficult to squeeze the innovative stuff into the category anymore. Not impossible—note Benford, Varley, Gotschalk, X, Y and Z—but hard as hell. Why bother, eh Carter? How can you—how can I—take it seriously anymore?

1979/1980: New Jersey

I Could Have Been a Contender
Part One

Revisionist canon now holds that science fiction would have had a different—and superior—history if Hugo Gernsback, by creating *Amazing Stories* in 1926, had not ghettoized the genre, reduced it on the spot to a small asylum plastered with murals of ravening aliens carrying off screaming women in wondrous machines from a burning city and thus made it impossible for serious critics, to say nothing of serious writers, to have anything to do with it. After all, in the early part of the century novels of the speculative and fantastic were part of the literature; the Munsey magazines ran futuristic adventure serials all the time, and Hawthorne and Melville were writing fantasies or absurdist speculation without any damage to their literary credibility.

It simply could have gone on that way, the revisionists suggest; science fiction would not have been thrown into a charnel house which it would spend four decades trying to escape, seeking that respectability and acceptance it had possessed before Gernsback defined it and made it live by its worst examples and most debased audience.

The argument has a certain winsome charm—I believed it myself when I was but a wee lad, and some of our best or better minds hold to it right now—but is flawed. At the risk of aligning myself with Hugo Gernsback, a venal and small-minded magazine publisher whose reprehensible practices, long since detailed, were contemptible to his contributors, partners and employees, I think that he did us a great service and that were it not for Gernsback, science fiction as we understand it would not exist. We would have—as we do—the works of fabulation in the general literature—Coover, Barthelme, Barth and DeLillo—but of the category which gave *More Than Human, The Demolished Man, Foundation and Empire, Dying Inside, The Dispossessed* and *Rogue Moon* we would have nothing, and hence these works would not exist. It is possible that some of these writers, who were inspired to write science fiction by a childhood of reading, would never have published at all.

"Science fiction builds on science fiction," Asimov said once, and that truth is at the center of the form. Before Gernsback gave it a name (he called it "scientifiction," but close enough; Ackerman a few years later cast out a syllable), the literature did not exist; before he gave it a medium of exclusivity, its dim antecedents were scattered through the range of popular and restricted writing without order, overlap or sequence. It was the creation of a label and a medium which gave the genre its exclusivity and a place in which it could begin that dialogue, and it was the evolution of magazine science fiction—slowly over the first decade, more rapidly after the ascension of Campbell—that became synonymous with the evolution of the field.

Only the rigor and discipline of the delimited can create art. Musicologists considering Bach, who worked within desperately restrictive format, will concur as will those considering the sonata form. The sonnet and the eight-bar chorus of almost all popular song and operetta give similar testimony. It was the very restraint with which science fiction was cloaked from the outset which gave the genre its discipline and force. Without the specialized format of the magazines, where science fiction writers and readers could dwell, exchange, observe one another's practices and build upon one another's insight, the genre could not have developed.

The first-generation science fiction writers—those whom Gernsback, Harry Bates and F. Orlin Tremaine brought into *Amazing* and *Astounding* after their small stock of recycled Wells and Verne had been used—worked under the most generalized influence and without canon: their work showed it. The second generation—those identified with Campbell—was composed of people who had grown up reading the early science fiction and were prepared to build upon it. The third generation, coming in the nineteen-fifties, was composed of writers who had correspondingly more sources and possibilities (and also a larger stock of ideas already proved unworkable or exhausted) and the increasing subtlety and complexity of the form through their years testifies once again to, as it were, the influence of influence . . . upon influence.

Science fiction, as John W. Campbell once pointed out expansively, may indeed outdo all of the so-called mainstream because it gathers in *all* of time and space . . . but science fiction as it has evolved is an extraordinarily rigorous and delimiting medium. Like the canon and the fugue, the sonnet and the sonata, like haiku, it has its rules, and the control of those rules is absolute. Extrapolative elements, cultural interface, characteriological attempt to resolve the conflicts between the two: *this* is science fiction.

The fact pervades all the decades after about 1935: no one could publish science fiction unless exposed to a great deal of it; virtually everyone who has ever sold a story has a sophisticated reader's background in the form, usually acquired just before or around adolescence. At the underside, this has led to parochialism, incestuousness and the preciosity of decadence (and there has been too much). In the end it may even be these qualities which finish science fiction off, make its most sophisticated and advanced examples increasingly inaccessible to the larger reading audience. But whatever happens to science fiction, it would not exist at all if it had not been given a name and a medium and for this, if we are not led to praise Gernsback, we must entomb him with honor. He was a crook, old Hugo, but he made all of us crooks possible.

1980: *New Jersey*

Anonymity & Empire

To the American literary community—to the American arts establishment—the science fiction writers of the forties were invisible. There is no more graceful way to put this. There were, for the first half of the decade, almost no books at all: no anthologies, no reprints, no second-serial rights. Novels and stories were written for genre magazines of limited circulation, were published and went out of print, presumably forever. Asimov has written that everything about his career after 1946 came as a surprise; he had no idea at the time he was writing "Nightfall," "Foundation" or the robotics series that this work would live beyond the issues of the magazines in which they appeared. This did not bother him (it might have bothered others) at all: what purpose did science fiction *have* except to live briefly and die forever in the magazines for kids? There was sufficient reward in becoming part of the ongoing literature. The Queens Science Fiction League was certainly not the world, but for the young Asimov its approval and awe were all that he could have asked.

It must be understood that in certain respects science fiction was no different for its writers, offered nothing less, than did the other branches of popular literature. It was pulp and appeared in the torrent of pulp magazines which by the hundreds got on in various degrees of health until wartime paper shortages and, finally, the curse of television put almost all of them in the ground by the beginning of the fifties. Western and romance writers, adventure and sports pulpeteers also worked for a half cent to two cents a word and knew that when the magazines went off sale their work would never be seen by a nonrelative or nonlover again. (Mystery writers did have a small book market but in the pre-Mystery Writers of America days only a vanishingly small percentage of magazine work could in expanded form find a book market—and advances, averaging around $250 even for first-rank writers like Woolrich, were an insignificant part of their income.) The difference between science fiction writers and those of the other pulp genres, however, was that science fiction writers took their work seriously, put far more into it psychically and were writing (because of the dominant presence of Campbell) to a consistently higher standard, an imposed rigor and specialized background. It was impossible, then as now, to write science fiction without the most intimate reading knowledge of the form, simply because the field was advancing so quickly in its language and devices that each story either made a direct contribution to the ongoing literature or risked rejection on the basis that it did not.

Surely—I defer to my sometime collaborator Bill Pronzini here with whom I have discussed the issue—western, romance, sports and certainly mystery writers might have been no less serious about their work, no less dedicated or professional. They certainly were not their inferiors technically, and the anonymity must have had profound effects upon them no less than upon the science fiction writers.

But almost all the science fiction writers were specialists. If they did not have a thorough working knowledge of the literature and the cutting edge, they did not survive. By 1940, very few of the science fiction writers who had been in *Astounding* prior to Campbell were still there; others had been thrown out and their names—Schachner, Schopeflin, Cummings—were legion. They had been evicted not through Campbellian malice but because they were either unable or unwilling to meet his editorial demands.

Campbell did better—felt that he had no alternative, really —by bringing in writers who had no sales background or alternate markets at all so that he could work with them from the outset . . . and because they had no alternate markets, they were less inclined to put up a battle against Campbell's demands.

Most of the pre-Campbell writers were pulp generalists who wrote through the entire range of fiction magazines and for whom science fiction constituted only a small percentage of output. Schachner and Arthur Leo Zagat, for instance, were enormously prolific and successful pulp writers; science fiction was only 10 percent of their output (and after their eviction less than that), but ironically they are remembered now only for their science fiction. Lester del Rey in his time did a fair amount for the confessions and sports magazines, but most of the first Campbell generation—Heinlein, Asimov, Sturgeon, de Camp—wrote little else. (The Kuttners under their own names and a plethora of pseudonyms wrote a great deal of fantasy but did not appear, as far as can be determined, to any extent in the other category magazines. The Kuttners, however, knew where to bury *all* the bodies.)

The rigor of the medium, demands of the market and the anonymity in which the work was done must have had their effect upon these writers. Asimov's feelings are known, but one can only surmise what science fiction did to the Kuttners, who were turning in work like "Vintage Season," "Mimsy Were the Borogoves," "Shock," "When the Bough Breaks" for a cent and a half a word; what science fiction did to van Vogt, who was turning out over two hundred thousand words of it a year working sixteen hours a day in a small apartment (and doing some confession stories too); what science fiction meant to Heinlein, who wrote *Sixth Column* for about $900 and "By His Bootstraps" and "Universe" for maybe $300 each—all of these writers putting out this work without an inkling that it would ever appear again or be read by other than the young core audience for the magazines.

In a sense this anonymity may have been liberating—one of the benefits of writing without a sense of posterity or audience may be a great and abounding freedom, the conviction that since what one is doing really does not matter one can, accordingly, do anything one wants—and the texts and commentaries of the time indicate that to a degree all the writers felt this way. It was a new kind of fiction being written in a different fashion; the knowledge that it was breakthrough literature of a sort might have been comforting to writers who could rationalize that what they did was too ambitious for a mass audience. Nonetheless, the record makes clear that almost all of this generation were finished by the end of the decade and looking for other things to do. Heinlein had turned (after a few stories for *Collier's* and *The Saturday Evening Post*, the first mass-magazine science fiction in decades) to the juvenile book market and was writing on contract for Scribner's with only a few "adult" novels—*The Puppet Masters, Double Star, The Door into Summer*—serialized in the magazines. L. Ron Hubbard with A. E. van Vogt and Katherine MacLean had disappeared into the Dianetics Institute, from which the latter two emerged to write again only a decade and a half later. L. Sprague de Camp turned to nonfiction, juveniles, and a scattering of fantasy and was a small factor in fifties science fiction. Asimov had taken a doctorate in biochemistry, and in 1949, after a few months of excruciating ambivalence, took a full-time teaching position at Boston University (the controlling aspect of his decision being that he had never made nor had any reason to believe that he could ever make a living from science fiction).*

The Kuttners had returned to school at USC, seeking undergraduate degrees in psychology and then going on to graduate work; Henry did a series of mysteries for Harper's but with the exception of "Humpty Dumpty" (finishing off the series published immediately thereafter by Ballantine as *Mutant*), never appeared in *Astounding* in the decade and only once in *Galaxy* (and once in *Fantasy and Science Fiction*). Del Rey and Sturgeon stayed in the hunt but changed their markets, Sturgeon publishing only one story in ASF in the

---

* Asimov reports that as of December 1949 he had received a total of slightly less than $12,000 for his entire output. Considering what Asimov had done and what his stature in the field was already by that time, there may be no need to say anything else about the forties in science fiction.

nineteen-fifties and del Rey a bare scattering. The creation
and expansion of the book market for science fiction, the restoration to print (in certain cases highly remunerative) of the
work written in anonymity must have been highly gratifying
to these writers, but it appeared to inspire none of them to
return to the steady production of science fiction. An entire
new generation—one could say several generations—of science
fiction writers were needed to pursue the vastly expanded category in the fifties and of course they presented themselves.
Among them were the finest writers who had ever worked in
the form, and collectively they gave science fiction its great
decade.

But the first Campbell generation did not play a significant
role in the science fiction of the fifties. Nor did Campbell: he
stayed behind, doing exactly as he had been doing; but science fiction had been taken from him and, as the decade
went on, surely he knew it. His magazine began to enact his
increasing bewilderment and recrimination. The price the
forties had imposed had been exacted; the battle had, long
after the fact, been won . . . but only after the writers had
ceased to fight. This late outcome from early and lonely
struggle must have been the true bitterness of the decade for these writers, and why so very few of them, although
relatively young long after the decade, were unable to reproduce their best work.

Anonymity is at least an openness of promise; outcome,
whatever it may be, is a weight upon the heart.

1980: New Jersey

I Don't Know How
to Put It Love
but I'll Surely Surely Try

Back in the innocent early seventies when it became a regular program item at the science fiction conventions, the panel on Sex and Science Fiction was a *draw*, guaranteed to get the audience not only awake but in motion before noon. That was a long time ago, to be sure; now the topic has subdivided like a maddened amoeba: fragmented into panels on Homophobia in Science Fiction, Feminism in Science Fiction, Stereotyped Images of Intercourse in Science Fiction, Phallic and Breast Imagery—it is quite enough to unsettle the mind of an aging man who grew up in this field on a diet of Catherine Tarrant's judiciously copy-edited *Astounding*. I can barely cope.

Nonetheless, writers being either sharply ahead or seriously behind their time (usually both and simultaneously), I am just about ready now to address the subject of sex in science fiction. It occurred to me sometime in 1976 that I had spent most of the decade up until then locked in a room typing, and when I stumbled out blinking it was with the feeling that I would have to be slowly and gently reacquainted with the world. The adolescent lunge as free after-care clinic. So it is the generality with which I must deal.

Most of my contemporaries have already had their say* on the issue (on the Sunday morning panels not unaided by raucous shouts from the audience and bottles of beer) and now

* And their due.

it is, as Clifford Irving did *not* entitle his "authorized" biography of Howard Hughes, My Turn.

Sex in science fiction. Well, then. Sex in the *literature* of science fiction? Or in the lives of the respective writers? Or—modesty makes one tremble—in the conventions and other social events of the field? These are significant topics, each of them, and together they induce a collective sense of woe. To deal with all within the space of a single essay not only would be an accomplishment of thundering magnitude but would be to take clinical depression to its next logical step, mania and the beginnings of acting out. A middle-aged suburbanite had best watch himself.

Accept delimitation, accept the Hemingway theory that the power comes not from what is said but what is *un*said; accept one's condition and discuss sex in the literature of science fiction.

One can inaugurate the conference by saying that until about 1952 in American genre science fiction there was none at all. There was heavily masked, coded, templated (that last, now fashionable academese) sex to be sure: aliens carrying off women in the pulp magazines, men carried off by or carrying off machines in *Astounding*; men beat up on one another quite a bit in all the publications and women stood in an odd relationship to technology, usually failing to understand it.

This undertext could be explained by the merest undergraduate in Psychology 5, Introduction to Human Development, but not until Philip José Farmer and Sam Mines conspired as author and editor to publish *The Lovers* and its semisequels in *Startling Stories* did sexuality as an important human drive having the power to motivate, enlighten, damage or dignify become incorporated into a genre which had already existed as a discrete subcategory for more than a quarter of a century, three hundred and twenty-five months of magazine issues, perhaps twelve thousand stories of varying lengths in which not once did anything resembling carnal knowledge occur onstage. Never.

Twenty-seven years of asceticism are not easy to deny in life as well as art. Carnality may whisk one through the barriers in an instant, but the implications often are not understood for many years. *The Lovers* was well-received—Mines, doubtless to his relief, got away with it clean and Farmer published a few semisequels (*Mother*, and *Open to Me My Sister*)—but matters otherwise remained unchanged. In 1958, Theodore Sturgeon was able to smuggle in cautious intimations of homosexuality and the polymorphous perverse, and nothing less than sexual passion is the lever that makes Budrys's *Rogue Moon* go, but as late as 1965, science fiction was still a genre which in the main denied the existence, let alone the extent, of human sexuality.

(It became a grim or frivolous game for some of the writers who were, of course, not fools, to see what they could slip by *without* editorial knowledge or consent. One famously was able to get through J. W. Campbell and Kay Tarrant a description of a tomcat as a "ball-bearing mousetrap" and Asimov's 1951 "Hostess" in *Galaxy* reeked of the perversity of sexual attraction between an alien diplomat and a repressed academic's wife but these triumphs were few and, more to the point, unnoticed. If they had attracted wide attention the writers would have paid the price.)

All of this began to end at last with Michael Moorcock's publication in the British *New Worlds*, to whose editorship he had acceded after Ted Carnell, of work by writers like Ballard and Aldiss and Langdon Jones which made frank use of sexual motifs. Two years later, in 1967, Harlan Ellison's *Dangerous Visions* delivered in the form of an original anthology thirty-three stories allegedly unpublishable in the magazine markets, almost half of them dealing with sexuality as the central theme. The book was successful and opened the way for many writers and anthologists who went and did likewise. In 1968 in *Galaxy*, Robert Silverberg was able to get "fuck you" into the sacrosanct pages by putting it in the binarese of a horny and demented computer. (In early 1970

Silverberg got The Word itself into *Galaxy* right after Harlan
Ellison put "shit" into *F & SF* and just before I slid "cock-
sucker" into *Fantastic*.†)

By the beginning of the nineteen-seventies, novels of great
or relative explicitness (Silverberg's *Dying Inside*, *The Second Trip* and *The World Inside*, my own *Beyond Apollo*)
bore the label of category science fiction. Short stories in original anthologies edited by Silverberg, Knight, Harrison and
Carr were also using sexual material. *Galaxy* continued to run
sexually explicit work and by the mid-seventies copulation
and masturbation had even made their way into Ben Bova's
Analog. By the start of the eighties, although the Promised
Land was not outside these windows last time I looked
(Moskowitz and I both know that the Promised Land was
sacked, looted and cleaned to the ground by 1938 at the latest), the science fiction writer, particularly the science fiction
novelist, began to deal with sexuality in the same freedom
that could be applied to technology, apocalypse, political
repression or bigotry a quarter of a century ago.

Why was sexuality so late in arriving? Why was the capacity to depict its full range in fact practically the *last* element
to reach the genre, long after it had become in all other ways
a viable literary medium?

The explanation is directly related to the general age of sf
readership. Science fiction has always been a genre the majority of whose readers are young. Perhaps nine tenths of them
are under twenty-five, close to 50 percent under sixteen. The
young are exposed to parental and social sanctions of the
most unpleasant sort. *Playboy* could break the distribution
patterns and drag hundreds of imitators through the mesh,
but the magazines (and until the sixties science fiction was a
magazine genre) were at the mercy of magazine distributors
whose wives and children (distributors being able neither to
read nor write) felt that science fiction was to be aseptic. The
covers were a sell but inside, where the truth lurked, the al-

† It takes a writer of real literary background and ambition to make a major
contribution like this.

iens' designs were simple and wholesome. They sought not to copulate but to kill.

Almost all science fiction published in book form prior to 1965 had appeared previously in the magazines, and almost all the science fiction therein was produced by writers and editors with at least an eye and a half on the whims of the magazine distributors who simply did not want to take chances with products which were (unlike the high-priced *Playboy*) marginally profitable, nickel-and-diming. One distributor pullout could topple a magazine; if the publisher had a chain his entire line might be endangered.

Accordingly, a kind of least common denominator applied to magazine science fiction: if a given story could be perceived as giving potential offense to anyone, it was the path of least resistance to reject or at least edit it heavily. Catherine Tarrant at *ASF* and Horace Gold at *Galaxy* notably did so. Under the circumstances, the remarkable fact was that *The Lovers* sold at all—and it did, of course, appear in one of the low-paying and marginal pulp magazines of its era, a magazine so endangered already that it went out of business (through no fault of Farmer) less than two years later.

Still and in sum it is now the eighties and science fiction has not only caught on, it has caught up. The dear old field has made all of the changes and is, in the view of many of its critics (not all of them aged), no less dirty than any other branch of modern literature. The critics mutter and murmur but many of their own icons, writers who were models of restraint, have fallen off the wagon in recent years and resolved to show Harlan Ellison and Langdon Jones a couple of things.

Isaac Asimov's *The Gods Themselves* has a central section which is about nothing if not exclusively sex, and Robert Heinlein's three most recent novels, *The Number of the Beast, Time Enough for Love* and *I Will Fear No Evil* are not only about sex but about sexual perversity and its endless lacunae; they are quarter-million-word investigations of subjects—transvestism, narcissism, autoeroticism, copulation—which even Hubert Selby, Jr., or Henry Miller would not treat so obsessively. (There are entire sentences in *Tropic of Cancer* which have nothing at all to do with sex. Selby in *Last Exit to Brooklyn* went on for *paragraphs*.)

On balance—the panel draws to a close, the participants look wearily at the clock and the audience is shuffling in place and waving hands; sorry, no questions folks, we can hardly bear to go on even when left to ourselves—the question of sex in science fiction is one which seems to have been resolved, by simple majority, in favor of sex. The issue is important now in historical, not textual, perspective.

And that is where the real critical work of the next half century is going to be done; it will address the bigger questions. To what degree did the practical taboos under which it functioned as a form of popular literature alter science fiction? Science fiction has been regarded by the universities for a long time as a debased if energetic form of popular literature—but how much of that debasement was *imposed* rather than intrinsic? To what degree, in fact, may science fiction be seen as victim rather than perpetrator of its greatest weaknesses? How much false characterization, contrived plotting, coy retreat, dissimulation was forced upon writers who were working in a field which made their work contemptible to them if they were to do it at all?

In short—and this is no small point—science fiction may not have been populated by bad writers or editors but by extraordinarily good examples who, functioning under taboos which would have destroyed those less capable, were able to do more than the distributors, the wholesalers *and the audience* ever suspected. Science fiction, viewed from this context, might be conceived as a kind of difficult tribute to the human spirit, a monument to cunning.

And then again, it might not. It would be easier perhaps to stand with and for the Kazins and Howes, Abrahams and Charyns to argue that it was (is!) junk about people without genitals for kids of all ages who could barely read or bear to think.

But I do not think so.

I think that in its damages lies its magnificence.

I think that in those necessities suspired the truth.

1979/1980: New Jersey

Memoir from Grub Street

I edited *Amazing Stories* and *Fantastic Stories*, bimonthly science fiction magazines, from April 1968 to October 1968; it was not the best of times but was hardly the worst either (although in my youthful exuberance I then thought it was). I was the magazines' only employee, edited them from my bedroom, delivered the copy-edited, blurbed manuscripts to the printer, proofed the galleys. Art and layout were handled by the publisher from *his* home, the publisher assuming more expertise in these areas (he had to be right) than I. Eventually, a dispute over control of the art—I commissioned a couple of covers but the publisher did not want to use them and I threatened to quit if he didn't—caused me to be fired by telephone on a Sunday afternoon just as the Giants were about to score a touchdown (prophetically they did not), but that is not the subject of this essay nor is my salary ($100 a month to start, merit increases up to $150 right before the end), nor is my self-image at the time as the logical successor to Hugo Gernsback, T. O'Conor Sloane, Raymond Palmer and Paul Fairman. I was *quite* young.

Amazing, after Ziff-Davis publishers precipitately dumped it and its miserable sister in 1965 because of declining sales (although their last editor, Cele L. Goldsmith, was certainly the best magazine editor extant then), had fallen upon desperate times; the publisher had acquired it, if not for a song, at least for a medley, and it was his hope to float it along by access to the magazine's backlist (Ziff-Davis had purchased all serial rights, granting unlimited reprint). Joseph Ross was his first editor, Harry Harrison unhappily the second and I ambivalently the third: only when Ted White began his ten-year stewardship and commenced to make real inroads on the publisher's obduracy did the publication or its companion have any impact again.

No, my editorship was of little moment and although I was able to find and publish some expert work (Lafferty's "This Grand Carcass," "Yet," Wodhams' *Try Again*, Richard C. Meredith's first novel, *We All Died at Breakaway Station*), I never thought of myself as much more than an adequate editor. I was able to separate good from bad and publish the better; this seemed the *minimum* requirement but I have subsequently learned that in contemporary publishing it is the last. My tenure was obviously too short to matter and the circulation of the magazines—possibly 24,000—would guarantee that whatever I did would be at the margins of a marginal field.

The real point of this reminiscence has to do with the submissions I faced and how they were handled, and it is this which might have relevance now. Consider the situation: *Amazing* and *Fantastic* were magazines at the bottom of the extant market. Unlike all the others, they paid on or after publication and, with a single exception (Tom Disch's literary agent fought like a trooper), paid a top rate of two cents a word. They were necessarily perceived by any writer at any level as publications to be placed on the absolute bottom of the list; I would see only what *Playboy*, *Analog*, *Galaxy*, *Worlds of If*, *Fantasy and Science Fiction*, *Venture* and *New Worlds* had rejected.*

Nonetheless, the magazines which at that time were publishing only 12,000 words of original material an issue—three stories of average length or a long novelette and a short one—received through the six months of my tenure an average of one hundred manuscripts a *week*. The scripts came from unknown and unpublished writers in preponderance, of

---

* Neither writers nor stories are machinery, of course, and it can be presumed that *Amazing* preempted in certain cases some of the markets on the list, but certainly I was seeing nothing on first submission.

course, but at least 25 percent of them, week after week, were signed by recognized names: some of them, like Leiber or Lafferty, at the top of the market as then constituted; others, like Wodhams, Koontz, Meredith or David R. Bunch, well in the middle range.

Most of the manuscripts were, to be sure, not publishable, but 15 percent of them (and more than half of those turned in by the professionals) were, and at least a third of that 15 percent, or five manuscripts a week, were outstanding. It is no exaggeration to recall that I received throughout my editorship sixty stories a month which by any standard I could ascertain were as good as or better than anything published in the competing magazines.

I was only able, because of space limitations, to buy perhaps twenty of those stories and perhaps another fifteen which were of lesser standard, which means that I rejected consciously about forty stories which were better than some I bought.† The word rate in all cases but that of Leiber and Disch was a penny a word on publication or shortly thereafter and all of the writers, every one of them, were glad to accept the terms. The stories were published, one of them (the Lafferty) was in a best-of-the-year collection and a couple more wound up in author collections.

The remainder vanished.

I think of this now and then, think of it in a time when the magazine market is even more constricted and when there are close to a thousand (instead of the five hundred) writers eligible for membership in the SFWA and at least some definition of professionalism. If sixty publishable short stories a *month* were of necessity being rejected by a bottom-line, penny-a-word market at *that* time, exactly what is going on now? *Worlds of If* and *Galaxy* are gone, *Amazing* under a new ownership is producing six issues a year (*Fantastic* is gone), *Venture* is gone, *Playboy* no longer does science fiction. *Omni* and *Isaac Asimov's* have appeared, of course, but the overall market is still in debit and there are almost

---

† You know the perversity of editors—or at least I do.

twice as many professional writers, to say nothing of the hordes of creative-writing majors of the seventies driven toward science fiction because the quality lit market no longer exists. And there are the usual host of science fiction fans/readers led naturally through their experience to attempt to write.

What is being lost now? How many stories in oblivion, how many careers unable to begin?

What can there be for all of these writers? The field needs—

Forget the field for the moment. We owe the field little at this point. What is the cost to these *people* of all of that failure and bitterness?

1980: New Jersey

The Fifties

Harry Harrison, who himself only got really going at the end, called the decade the false spring of science fiction, and Robert Sheckley, whose active early career corresponded almost exactly with the decade, shook his head when we talked about it in 1973 and said, "Well, I squeezed a couple of happy years at the beginning, anyway." James Gunn got a portion of his master's thesis into one of the fifty magazines that were published at some point during those years and at least twenty science fiction writers, it might have been forty, were making an accountant's wage from their trade. By 1960 it was all gone and it was five bleak years and another country before science fiction began to look hopeful again. Now, although some of the writers are still puttering around (and some like Fred Pohl, A. J. Budrys and Alfred Bester are having significant new careers) it all seems at a great remove—surely as frozen in time, as historical to the younger writers of this day, as the early Gernsback era seemed to my generation. And most of the work, most of the writers, need rediscovery. Many will surely never achieve it.

What happened? A lot happened. The historical theory of synchronicity was demonstrated at the end of the decade as never elsewhere before the era of the assassinations began. When it happens, it all happens together, in short. The massive American News Service (ANS), responsible for magazine distribution, was ruled a monopoly and into forced divestiture. Twenty magazines perished in 1958, and the sales of the leaders were halved. These magazines could not reach the newsstands in sufficient numbers. The audience could not find them. But the audience had already diminished; it had never been large enough to support more than a few successful magazines, a few continuing book lines, and Sputnik in 1957 had made science fiction appear, to the fringe audience, bizarre, arcane, irrelevant. There were dangerous matters going on now in near space but the sophisticated, rather decadent form which genre science fiction had become had little connection with satellites in close orbit.

And other things. Henry Kuttner and Cyril M. Kornbluth died within a month of each other in early 1958. Kuttner, one of the five major figures of the previous decade,* had left science fiction but was constantly reprinted and was only forty-four. Kornbluth, a decade younger, was indisputably at the top rank. These sudden, shattering deaths—one from a heart attack in sleep, the other from a stroke or heart attack—made a number of their contemporaries question the very sense of their careers. What had all of this gotten Kuttner and Kornbluth? "I was only twenty-three, then," Silverberg said, "but I somehow realized right away that these two men had literally died from writing science fiction and I was afraid that I was going to die too. I had some bad months." Dead, these writers, after ten or twenty years in the word-rate-on-acceptance mills.

By 1959, Anthony Boucher, editor of *The Magazine of Fantasy and Science Fiction*, had decided to join his founding coeditor, J. Francis McComas, in the semiretirement of free-lancing and H. L. Gold was getting out too. Gold, editor of *Galaxy*, had been literally paralyzed by war-induced agoraphobia; unable to leave his apartment or carry on the semblance of a normal social life, he had been deteriorating for many years, and a period of hospitalization (on a rare, terrified sally out of doors he was struck by a car) convinced him that he could continue editing no longer. Fred Pohl had

---

* The others, for the record, were Robert Heinlein, Isaac Asimov, A. E. van Vogt and L. Sprague de Camp.

already been running the magazine ex officio; he took over the title too. And by 1959 only a few steady book markets for science fiction remained. Unplanned, imitative overproduction for an audience imagined larger than it was, the curse of science fiction publishing then as now, had resulted in many publishing catastrophes and only Ace, Doubleday and Ballantine remained as steady outlets for all but the very few writers such as Heinlein and Clarke who had broken out of the category.

John W. Campbell at *Astounding* had wandered from Dianetics to the Hieronymus Machine to the finagle factor and was just beginning to topple into Norman Dean's Drive, meanwhile running stories by a few writers functioning under innumerable pseudonyms with virtually the same plot, conception, characters and outcome. Only Rick Raphael (who was gone by 1965) seemed to be able to break into and sell interesting work to *ASF* in those years; Campbell had no other new writers of any visible promise.

An unhappy, airless time. An end of time for many. So emphatically hopeless that when science fiction began to pick up once more in the mid-sixties, first with the British *New Worlds* and then with the fusion of new writers, new approaches in the barbarous colonies themselves, a new audience was unaware of what had been accomplished in the fifties and talked of the field's "new literary merit," "new relevance," "new excitement," "new standards of contemporaneity" as if nothing innovative had occurred before Ballard or Silverberg. Yet, as that second and less significant false spring of the late sixties and seventies also ebbs, the true dimensions of the fifties reappear, however distantly, across the murky waters. Time to reconsider.

Some historical background: at the end of the nineteen-forties, science fiction accounted for perhaps fifty books, hardcover and paperback, published commercially in a year. The field supported perhaps seven magazines, only one of which, *Astounding*, paid decent word rates (two cents a word on acceptance) or was read by other than a juvenile audience. Five years later, there were forty magazines fighting for space on the newsstands, hardcover and paperback novels and collections were coming out at the rate of two to three hundred a year and one book editor, Donald A. Wollheim at Ace, was publishing more science fiction in a month than had appeared in all of 1943. *The Magazine of Fantasy and Science Fiction*, appearing first in late 1949 and *Galaxy*, the first issue dated October 1950, were well-financed, carefully edited projects intended to offer *Astounding* serious competition, and by the inclusion of a wider range of style and thematic approach they sought an expansion of the audience itself. They succeeded at once—*Galaxy* was to outsell *Astounding* almost from its inception through the next five years; *Fantasy and Science Fiction*, beginning as a quarterly *Magazine of Fantasy*, went bimonthly and added sf within a year and then, as its natural audience found it, became a monthly in early 1952—and behind them, entrepreneurs picking up the scent, came a clutch of magazines. Some, like *Cosmos, Space* or *Rocket Stories*, lasted only a few issues, others like *Worlds of If* or *Science Fiction Adventures* held through various ownerships for longer, but through 1958 although magazines would collapse, new ones would spring. The growth of the field in a spectral minute was remarkable. In 1953 there were forty or fifty times the outlets for science fiction that had existed five years earlier.

Writers who had struggled with varying degrees of success through the bleak, building years—Sturgeon, Blish, Simak—found to their astonishment that they could almost make a living. A new generation of writers who had grown up under the influence of the Campbell decade were able to leap from late adolescence into full-time free-lance writing careers: Budrys, Sheckley, Dick, Gunn, Knight. The enormous expansion of the market was further signified by the fact that the three most prolific writers of the forties, Asimov, L. Ron Hubbard and van Vogt, backed away from science fiction to go into other careers† and that Heinlein, working on a long series of successful quasijuveniles for Scribner, abandoned short stories entirely as did L. Sprague de Camp, who concentrated on nonfiction.

It was a pretty good time for Francis E. Walter, General Motors, Mitch Miller's Columbia Records popular division and science fiction alike. Some of the field's historians (notably Fred Pohl in a 1975 essay "Golden Ages Gone Away") do not see these factors as unrelated; *Galaxy* and *Fantasy and Science Fiction* were among the very few mass markets where, sufficiently masked, an antiauthoritarian statement could be published. There are rumors of professors and engineers trapped in the academies or industry who turned to the science fiction magazines and both read and wrote for them (pseudonymously) avidly as absolutely the *only* medium where the policies and procedures of the late Senator Joseph McCarthy were explicated fully and mocked. Cyril M. Kornbluth in a 1957 symposium spoke of the hundreds of people in advertising who had thanked him and Fred Pohl in desperation for publishing the only novel, *The Space Merchants*, that told the truth about their industry and what it wanted the world to be. (Kornbluth added characteristically that of course, for all these thanks and testimonials, the novel had not changed its target medium to the slightest degree: advertising was exactly what it had been and so, to be sure, was Cyril Kornbluth.)

One has to continue, however, by discussing what kind of work was being done to occupy the space that the publishers in their enthusiasm or simple greed had created. Say this at the outset: there has only been a trickle of novels through the fifty-five-year history of science fiction that have been consensually accepted as masterpieces, absolute examples of what the field can be at its best. With no exception that I can

---

† Asimov continued to appear in the magazines with diminishing frequency through the first half of the decade, but even the five or six serialized novels and fifty short stories represented a sharp cutback and the stunning expansion of the market diffused his proportionate impact. "Editors missed me a bit," he wrote laconically about the period.

glimpse, *all* of them were published in the fifties. The jury on the seventies is, by definition, still out (it looks as if *Dying Inside*, *The Dispossessed*, perhaps 334 and *Shadrach in the Furnace* and *The Ocean of Night* may make it), but there is virtually no novel of the sixties, however acclaimed in its time, which does not have a substantial and influential claque in opposition, as it did then.‡ Forties novels of significance: *Slan*, *Final Blackout*, *Sixth Column*, *World/Players of Null-A*, *Fury* look archaic now: primitive and unfulfilled. They have fallen out of print; the most recently reissued of them, the Kuttner's *Fury*, has not appeared since 1973. (That non-novel, *The Martian Chronicles*, *does* have a good in-print record but Bradbury has had for decades access to the audience outside the genre and the television production has been a spur.)

Consider, though, the fifties. A *Canticle for Leibowitz*, *More Than Human*, *Double Star*, *Rogue Moon*, *The Space Merchants*, *Gladiator-at-Law*, *The Demolished Man*, *The Stars My Destination*, A *Case of Conscience*, *Bring the Jubilee*. (All are currently in print except for *Gladiator-at-Law*.) *Rogue Moon* won no awards; *Canticle* was published in its year. Kornbluth's *The Syndic* copped no honors; *More Than Human* in that year. To consider that *The Demolished Man*, *The Space Merchants* and *Baby Is Three* (the central section of *More Than Human* from which the fore and aft of the novel were flung) all appeared in *Galaxy* within a nine-month period in 1952 is to be awed.

Novels, of course, collect the attention, the reissues and occasionally the money (*The Space Merchants*, despite recent enormous advances to Silverberg, Heinlein and Gregory Benford, may still be, over its twenty-nine-year life, the most remunerative of all genre science fiction novels) but science fiction, unlike any other category of literature, lives in the short forms. The short story or novelette seem perfectly avail-

‡ *Bug Jack Barron*, *Stand on Zanzibar*, *Dune*, *The Left Hand of Darkness*, *Black Easter*, *Thorns*, *The Moon Is a Harsh Mistress*, *Camp Concentration*; case rests.

able to the articulation and enactment of a single speculative conceit which, one could insist, is the task for which science fiction itself is most suited. The level of short-story writing during the decade in technical expertise and inventiveness has never been equalled nor have *any* short stories published within the last fifteen years had the impact upon the field and its audience of what was appearing routinely in the best-of-the-year anthologies or magazine anthologies. Until the advent of John Varley in 1975, no short story writer in two decades sprang upon science fiction as did Mark Clifton through *Astounding*.

There is probably no way in which to teach a young audience (eighty percent of science fiction readers are under twenty) that Mark Clifton, dead a long time and virtually out of print, was for a period of four years the most controversial and influential writer in the magazines. No way to teach them that Floyd L. Wallace, *Galaxy's* Clifton who published novelettes of increasing inventiveness and technical clarity, also virtually unreprinted although alive, taught at least one writer what the conceptual limits of the science fiction novelette might be. No way to teach them that the short stories of Damon Knight and Alfred Bester, in their technical ease and ambition, struck not only readers but professionals of their own and the previous generation as miraculous—miraculous that such work could be both recognizably genre science fiction and of indisputable artistic quality. (Knight and Bester collections are available; between them, however, they have not published a dozen new stories in as many years.)

One of the hazards, not to say horrors, of age is the reconsideration of our youthful selves, the vision of subsequent heartbreak superimposed, the memory of what we became shading inexorably what we took ourselves to be. The conclusion must come that we were fools and it is this, perhaps, which has left the fifties almost bereft of significant critical reevaluation and comment. Those suited lived through the time and still feel the pain. They were naïve. They wrote themselves a bill of goods and hawked it and bought it, every rotten, self-delusory item. Sure they know it now. They knew it by 1959 and it destroyed some of them. But the bill of goods seemed reasonable.

It really did. It appeared possible to remake the field. By the end of the forties, Campbell and his contributors had put the technical equipment of the modern short story, the rigors of scientific extrapolation into the hands of those ready to begin where the rest, through struggle, had finally peaked. Hiroshima and television, the cold war and the mass market had delivered unto the new writers and editors what appeared to be an enormous audience for a kind of fiction that would truly come to terms with the potential changes in lives caused by new and virtually controllable technology.

Horace Gold earnestly believed that *Galaxy* could eventually appeal to as many people as *The Saturday Evening Post*. Boucher and McComas, world-weary types, had less evangelistic obsession and more cynicism, but saw no reason why the audience for literate science fiction should be any smaller than that for fiction itself.* These major editors and John W. Campbell who was, at his worst, not *impervious* to good writing (a story would not, at least, be rejected for literary quality if it did not lack more immediate Campbellian virtues) gathered about them fifty to a hundred writers who, demoniacally inspired, were willing to try to take the field to the limit of their abilities, knowing that whatever they did they would not be rejected for trying too hard. These writers could not, of course, sell the major editors everything, but they could write passionately and often and the overflow, much of high quality, was being laid off to those thirty or forty magazines which appeared and disappeared like Flying Dutchmen.

(A few magazines such as *Infinity* or *Venture* or, at the be-

---

* The payoff which Boucher, perhaps fortunately, did not live to see is that there is now in mass-market terms almost no audience for quality fiction at all, a fact not unnoted by science fiction editors—not, on balance, a dumb group.

ginning of the decade, *Worlds Beyond*, were created for the specific purpose of publishing a more literate and stylistically ambitious, thematically uncomfortable kind of science fiction, and these magazines were not publishing rejects so much as working on direct commission. They all failed, and except for *Infinity* failed quickly, but who in 1960 or 1981 would consider for the mass market a magazine devoted to the publication of non-mass-market fiction?)

It was a period which had never before occurred in mass-market fiction, perhaps in fiction of any kind. There was a wide market *and* one of exceeding range; work of quality was as readily acceptable within the confines of the genre as less ambitious science fiction. *Black Mask* and some of the other detective pulp magazines of the thirties had had no prejudice against art and had published Dashiell Hammett, Raymond Chandler and Cornell Woolrich, but there were many more science fiction magazines and (*pace* Pronzini) more genuinely gifted science fiction writers in the fifties than mystery writers in the thirties. But almost *any* writer who had a decent reading knowledge of the genre and could reproduce it to minimum standard could find a market. Thirty magazines times eight stories a month times twelve meant close to three *thousand* science fiction stories published a year, to say nothing of the original anthologies: *Star Science Fiction, Star Short Novels* and *New Tales of Space and Time.* (Today magazines and original anthologies together accommodate perhaps three hundred new stories a year.) In 1955 there were in the United States and England perhaps two or three hundred writers who had managed some degree of professionalism. (Today there are over a thousand.) And the book market was not negligible. Wollheim was at Ace, Doubleday had begun a small program, Simon & Schuster were committed to a dozen titles a year, Signet, Avon and Pocket Books were toe in the water and Ballantine, beginning a flourishing program in 1953 with *The Space Merchants*, started by offering advances of five thousand dollars.

Magazine rates were about what they are now. The top magazines paid three to five cents a word, the middle range one and a half to two, the bottom rarely less than a penny. In New York (or anywhere) at that time it was possible for a family to live with passable adequacy on five thousand dollars a year, comfortably on twelve. One without a family could get by on half that. It was not at all difficult to make five hundred dollars a month writing science fiction.

Five hundred dollars a month was, perhaps figuring in the rejects and aborted stories, twenty-eight thousand words for a professional, and twenty-eight thousand words a month is a thousand a day with most Sundays off. A thousand words a day fall on three typewritten pages: some bleed more than others, of course, but three pages are nevertheless three pages (and no true professional will ever admit to an editor or even his peers how very quickly they can be done, particularly under pressure). There was more than enough time for bull sessions conspiring on plans for the field, drinking sessions ditto, club meetings, travel, conferences, parties and the exchanging of wives. (These were not wife swappers, the male writers, they were wife *exchangers*. They would divorce and remarry. Members of this generation were perhaps the last to bend to the so-called new morality; they would rather marry than burn.)

The feeling in this rather insulated and socially peripheral circle of writers and their editors was that piece by piece they were remaking not so much the world (Auschwitz, Buchenwald, Dresden, Hiroshima, Joseph McCarthy had proved exactly what effect the seers and poets would have on the political and social reality of their time) but the field, that science fiction was being at last reconstructed toward that idealized form it might have attained a long time ago if Hugo Gernsback had not, for cynical publishers' reasons, slammed it into a format of bizarre adventures or marvelous inventions for kids and potential engineers.

Certainly the best of the magazine work was equal technically to the best of American fiction.† Kornbluth's "The Altar at Midnight," Bester's "The Men Who Murdered Mohammed," "Fondly Fahrenheit," "Hobson's Choice," "They Don't Make Life Like They Used To," Wallace's "Delay in Transit," Clifton's "Clerical Error," Pohl's "The Knights of Arthur" or "The Tunnel Under the World" and Sheckley's "Warm" (these titles are plucked virtually at random, sheer stream-of-consciousness; there are hundreds at this level, many by writers less well-known) were as accomplished and moving as "The Country Husband," "For Esme with Love and Squalor," "In the Zoo," "Among the Dangs," "Venus, Cupid, Folly and Time" or "The Man Who Studied Yoga."‡

There was, however, a tiny little problem.

Neither these stories nor the novels were recognized outside of the field at all. They made no impression. Outside of genre science fiction they did not, in fact, exist.

This failure of science fiction to reach outside its immediate audience was not of itself among the factors which blew away the false spring, but it might have been the factor that underlay everything. Science fiction remained small. It remained a small field. The audience upon which it could draw was perhaps half a million souls who were being asked to support their forty magazines and three hundred books, and with all their dedication they were too limited in numbers and too strapped for funds to do it. Most of them, after all, were kids. On allowances.

† And it is important to point out that science fiction in the fifties was a magazine field: almost everything originated there. The book publishers fed off what had been and was running in the periodicals, and only the bottom-line houses, like Monarch, published much nonmagazine material and that simply because these books were too weak to have achieved serial sale. The fifties novels mentioned earlier had *all* appeared originally in the magazines and most of them were commissioned and directed by the editors.

‡ This is not quite fair. Although "Among the Dangs" appeared first in *Esquire,* it was a science fiction story which was reprinted in *Fantasy and Science Fiction* and several genre anthologies. But if it had appeared *first* in *F & SF* it surely would not have won second (or even 980th) prize in the 1959 O. Henry Awards.

This core audience which perceives science fiction as important and to some degree necessary to their lives has never really increased from this half a million since the late forties. This is the central reason for the boom and bust phenomenon, as overextension inevitably hit the wall imposed by a readership which would not expand. The only difference between the fifties and the present, perhaps, is that the fringe audience—those who can be induced to buy two or three given titles a year through word of mouth, movie publicity or intense promotion—has expanded to several million. No science fiction novel in the fifties sold more than a hundred thousand paperback copies. Science fiction itself was regarded with disinterest or contempt outside the walls. Its very audience was an unorganized constituency; they were not in the main evangelical (in fact, like many of the academics, they were secretive), and those who were simply fed the popular perception of science fiction as a strange field: bizarre, endlessly incestuous and utterly defensive.

The genre made no impression upon the academic-literary nexus which controls critical perception (and eventually for serious writers may even create a large audience) in this country. Only two stories from the decade were reprinted in Martha Foley's *Best American Short Stories* annual: Sturgeon's "The Man Who Lost the Sea" and Judith Merril's "Dead Center." (Both from *Fantasy and Science Fiction*.) None ever appeared in the O. Henry Prize Stories. Not a story from *Galaxy, Astounding, Worlds of If, Worlds Beyond, Venture* or *Infinity* achieved even the thin gruel of the Foley roll of honor. (Some writers at the fringes of the field who published work in the quarterlies did make the Foley or O. Henry volumes, increasing the sense of injustice for the committed science fiction writers.)

No science fiction writer other than Ray Bradbury, that non-science fiction writer, appeared in textbooks. No science fiction novels other than Bradbury's were reviewed outside the genre departments of the press, gray caverns of brief notation. Most were ignored. *The Demolished Man* was published in hardcover by Shasta, a semiprofessional house operated by thieves, presumably because no reputable publisher wanted it.* *The Space Merchants* stayed in print but *Gladiator-at-Law* and *Wolfbane* did not.

By 1958, death and divestiture rolled around; the genre had been gutted. Many of its best writers were burnt-out cases. Aware of the anonymity of their work and lives outside of the small enclosure, aware of the necessity to go on and on just as they had simply to make an ever more difficult living, most either could or would write no longer. Probably if ANS had not been torn apart or Horace Gold had stayed together the field would have collapsed anyway. An entire generation of writers had been used up in the struggle to make science fiction a reputable literary medium. They had won—the evidence is there—and they had learned that for all the world cared they might not have bothered at all. They had made a living but an equivalent effort in insurance or the universities would have paid more and extracted less and the money was all gone anyway. Some of these writers have done no work for decades now. Others have done no good work. A couple have reemerged as if from behind barricades, hurled a couple of stories into the editorial mills and run for their lives again (often cut down by flying rejections).

A very, very few, Pohl, Bester and Budrys being the best examples, have returned to do outstanding work but only after a sabbatical of many years, and then at a slow rate. Between *Rogue Moon* (1959) and *Michaelmas* (1978) Budrys published one minor novel and a couple of short stories. He might have been the best of them; he certainly had the most profound, subtle mind, the best insight, the darkest perspective.

Gone, then. All gone away. After the energy of the late sixties to early seventies there came another slack period, a return to traditional themes and approaches, editorial hostility toward or bewilderment at stylistic or thematic innovation.

---

* Bester confirms this speculation in a 1980 essay for *Galaxy: 30 Years of Innovative Science Fiction*, published by Playboy Press.

Not to complain particularly: Varley has gotten through and Benford and Tiptree did or are doing major work. One can postulate that things will turn around eventually: new writers, new publishers, new editors . . . maybe a different politic and of course a new audience.

But virtually all the great innovators of the decade will carry on their work, careers and lives as if the fifties generation had never written. They will not know the work. That work may live in the undertext of the field, influence piled atop work influenced by the canon, but these writers will not know to whom they owe what. That decade, already done for for more than twenty years, will for most intents and purposes appear to have been for naught.

Was it?

Each generation, Donald Wollheim once said, has its own tragedy, must learn again on its own what every generation had had to learn and can never teach. Betrayal, circumstance, defeat. The Loyalists, the Cold War. Vietnam. And end broken in silence. There is no answer to any of this.

But *pace*, Gertrude, we may take up the question.

Yes. I think it was for naught.

1977/1980: New Jersey

The Fifties:
Recapitulation and Coda

Philip Klass's savage "The Liberation of Earth" appeared in Robert Lowndes' *Future Science Fiction.* Any history of the decade in science fiction must draw attention to this; if nothing else it will work against undue sentiment or self-delusion. *Future* was one of the longer-lived of the thirty or forty magazines that were born to perish within the decade; it paid a penny a word (less to unknown writers) around or after publication and had a circulation of, at the most optimistic estimate, thirty thousand as opposed to the one hundred that *Galaxy* or *Astounding* achieved at least intermittently. (And to keep all of this in perspective, let us recall that *The Saturday Evening Post* had a circulation of seven million and *Playboy*, starting from Hefner's garage in 1953, had exceeded two million by 1957. Science fiction then as now was a small field.)

"The Liberation of Earth," perhaps the most sophisticated antiwar story ever to appear in science fiction (my own late-sixties "Final War" and Effinger's "All the Last Wars at Once" from that period were little more than filigrees or variations; Haldeman's 1970s *The Forever War* harked back further than that), and a story which has subsequently been reprinted often enough to be Klass's best-known story after "Child's Play," this story appeared, in other words, in a bottom-line pulp magazine of negligible budget, circulation or influence, presumably—this is the safest of blind guesses—because none of the higher paying markets wanted any part of it whatsoever and because magazine editors outside of science fiction could not even take it seriously. All those aliens and tentacles and sucking air you know. Really weird stuff, Edmund. Kids say the darndest things.

There are many similar cases. Here are just a few: Blish's "Work of Art" and "Common Time," Kornbluth's "The Last Man Left in the Bar" and "Notes Leading Down to the Disaster," Knight's "Anachron," Margaret St. Clair's "Short in the Chest," Asimov's "The Last Question." All of these stories appeared in second and third line magazines. It is well understood that as the tragic Kornbluth became better and better his work drifted from *Astounding, Galaxy* and even *Fantasy and Science Fiction.* His last appearance in Campbell's magazine was in 1952 (with a novelette, *That Share of Glory* and the Judith Merril collaboration, *Gunner Cade*), and although collaborations with Fred Pohl appeared in *Galaxy* up to and beyond the end, his single byline was absent after the 1952 *Altar at Midnight. The Syndic,* perhaps his best novel, was rescued for serial publication by Harry Harrison for the staggering *Science Fiction Adventures.* Theodore Sturgeon appeared frequently in *Galaxy* through 1958 but not nearly so frequently in *F & SF* and with a single exception ("Will You Walk?" in January 1956) not at all in *Astounding.* And Mark Clifton, who had been Campbell's most renowned contributor between 1952 and 1955, sold only a five-hundred-word essay to *ASF* after the appearance of "Clerical Error" in the February 1956 issue. His last short stories and novel appeared in *Amazing.*

The point of this grim, pointilistic subhistory is that although the fifties were indeed a period of growth, optimism and experimentation for science fiction writers and readers, they were also characterized by the caution and terror which prevailed elsewhere. As the decade wandered in its sad and predictable way through the shores of political repression and public indifference, science fiction, no less than popular music or the products of General Motors, began to initiate decadence. (Defined most satisfactorily as being the elevation of form over function.) In a 1972 article by Gerald Jonas in

The New Yorker, Robert Silverberg remembered why in 1959 he abandoned science fiction for several years. The magazine collapse of the late fifties had left few markets. Silverberg observed, "One of them would let you say only cheerful things about science. Another would only let you say downbeat things about science. And the others wouldn't let you say anything at all."

The fifties was a festival—historians are yet to uncover its riches but they will—but it is important to note that in the festival's wake was left (carnival people know exactly what I mean) an empty landscape, much litter, a few lives not undamaged, a lot of bills not paid and heavy recriminations for those who had tried their luck at the wheel or with the fat lady or had carried their convictions too high for the dazzling night. The editors who lasted out the decade, Gold and Campbell, had become locked into parodies of their original editorial personas (paranoia and psionics) and Anthony Boucher had departed. Campbell pitched the tents of transcendence but by 1959 only the freak show seemed to draw his attention; Gold's shell game was rigorous but he had turned into a simple cheat. Cynical contributors knew by 1957 that they could sell Gold by toying deliberately with his agoraphobia and contributors equally cynical (there was some overlap) knew that the way into *ASF* was to make John Campbell himself the hero of a narrative. Meanwhile, *F & SF* had started a sexed-up companion, *Venture* (Kornbluth's last great story, "Two Dooms," was published there as was Walter Miller's strong "Vengeance for Nikolai," but the magazine nonetheless folded quickly), magazines were expiring in clumps and Philip Klass and A. J. Budrys had decided that the universities or the editorial desk were steadier and less humiliating than attempting to do serious work for editors who did not want it or readers who could not tell the difference. Many writers plain broke down, others were incapable of selling in a rapidly diminished market and were driven out. The fifties ended dismally for most science fiction writers. There is no other way to put this.

Still the work remains and is beginning to be looked over again. In the extreme long run* it will probably be ascertained that science fiction became both an art and contributed most of its best examples during the decade. The quality of even the top 20 percent was very high, higher than it had been before, higher than it is now.

What do not remain are the writers.

Very few of the major figures of the decade can be said to have had significant careers after 1960, and the few that have, significantly, stopped writing for quite a while. Pohl and Budrys became editors and only began to write science fiction in quantity again in the seventies, Alfred Bester became an editor at *Holiday* and was flat out from 1962 to 1975. Katherine MacLean and Theodore Sturgeon were little heard from in the sixties; Gordon Dickson and Poul Anderson carried on but Dickson had only begun to achieve prominence at the very end of the decade (*Dorsai!* in 1959 was his first noncollaborative novel), and Anderson, a persistent, stubborn professional, must be commended as the sole exception to prove the rule.

The decade itself burned out these writers, one might speculate. On the other hand—to be judicious—decades burn writers out simply by *being* decades; the working span of a creative literary career seems for most of us to be around ten years. One does not want to make the sociologist's error of retrospectively constructing a system that simply was not perceived at the time. There are, as has been pointed out, no literary movements, merely a bunch of writers sometimes hanging out together and trying to do their work.

And yet—ambivalence is the currency here—science fiction writers and editors are an incestuous bunch. Historically this is a close field. In this paradigm individual assent to circumstance was multiplied.

So let us not idealize. It offered much but was a bad time. Golden ages, all of them, look like brass from the inside; only the survivors call them golden and then because retrospective

---

* Lord Keynes early had the late word on this.

falsification is not only the sociologist's but the human condition. It was a hard time. It was a hard time, folks: good work got rejected, careers got broken, writers lost their way, marriages lost their way, editors lost their way, the country lost its way. The fifties set us up for disaster; by the end almost any breath of energy would have felt good even if it was to lead us to the fire. For my children the fifties are the Fonz and *Grease*, a loveable time; to me they are Francis E. Walters and McCarthy, the Rosenbergs and Jenner, the House Un-American Activities Committee and Richard M. Nixon. Still, Presley blew them open and Bester wrote like the divine. It is a mystery.

1979/1980: New Jersey

Ah Tempora! Ah Portions!
Ah Mores! Ah Outlines!

Typically—since the late nineteen-fifties when book publishers began to dominate the science fiction market—the science fiction novel has been written on portion and outline. The writer produces the first two or three chapters and a fairly detailed outline of the remainder of a novel (established writers may get away with less than that) and either directly or through an agent offers the material around. If it is sold, the writer gets a contract giving him the first half of the advance on signature of the contract, the remainder on delivery of the completed manuscript. (Some publishers cut the amount into thirds, the last due on publication, and others delay delivery payment until publication, but these are the exceptions and most professionals do not have to stand for it.)

One can theorize that this system is the single important factor underlying the science fiction of the last decades and may explain why almost all science fiction novels fail on a literary, artistic or structural level (if not all three).

Consider the writer. Consider his condition. He has produced, perhaps, ten thousand words on the basis of which he has been paid half the total amount due. Maybe he is modestly famous or knows the editor well; call it four thousand words on paper. These words were typed months or even years before the contract. He is now faced with the necessity to write in effect an entire book for half an advance (one tends to consider spent the signature advance upon its receipt—never existed). He has not thought of his book in months or years; it is already detached; he has only the vaguest recollection of characters, incident and plot and yet— ah, here it is—the book is due in not more than six months and nothing to be done but to write it for exactly half the money that the publisher knows it to be worth. The alternative is to return the advance (unthinkable) or simply not deliver and wait out the publisher, but although respectable careers in this field have been built upon nondelivery there are only a few available at any given time and even these have a cutoff point. Publishers have a stuffy tendency to go to court. Sooner or later even the weariest of us, the most venal or duplicitous must either write or get a job. (Well, one *could* farm out the manuscript to a struggling or unknown writer to ghost it under one's name for the delivery money and it's been done. But usually you need the money yourself and there is always the problem of exposure, that is if the delivery is at all publishable. There have been horrifying examples of the opposite.)

Here is the writer. He is thirty-two or twenty-seven or perhaps forty-six years old; his being groans with resentment, his skull is drained of last year's ideas. He hates the bastards for exploiting him and well he should because they are and do. Here too is the portion and outline. Particularly the outline.

It is, as such things usually are, chock-a-block with incident, color, character, motivation, conflict, metaphor, pizazz and fire. *Give them anything* may be the trade secret, but promise them a partridge in a pear tree. By the twelfth day of Christmas. In fact, promise it by the tenth. What will the stupid bastards remember by the time the chips are down and the advance is paid?

Here as well are the opening chapters. Carefully, patiently worked out they glint with promise, tumble with plot, glow with the dark and richly hued colors of invention. The time machine has jeweled dials, it has never before run so smoothly: automatic levers, brakes and protectors to guide against temporal paradox. The protagonist's lady friend is blonde and promising, but in her quieter moods the stranger aspects of her history emerge. The first scene between them reeks with implication and then there is that underground working to create the forces of paradox and brooding over *this* a somber, rigorous God . . .

God, the writer says. Sometimes he drinks. Often he proceeds to write. Sometimes he continues to write. Every now and then he simply writes and writes to get the thing over with; like Mark Twain's laziest preacher in the world who gave such long sermons because he got started and was too lazy to stop, it is often easier simply to get through the whole thing. Drop the blonde by the side, jettison her for good in Chapter 8, make the temporal paradox underground a figment of the protagonist's paranoia by Chapter 12. Move those levers, spin those dials, get the damned thing back to 2214 and write the final confrontation. But get it out of the house. It is forty-five thousand words, not the contracted sixty thousand, but with all the dialogue and wide margins who the hell will know the difference? Anyway, the word from the agent is that the commissioning editor, the gullible fool, was thrown out three months ago and his contract novels are now going directly to the copy editor, who will place *The Time Wizards of Lucidar* between a gothic and historical. *She* knows nothing about science fiction; why the hell should she? No one in the house except for the commissioning editor knew anything about science fiction and he's been fired, and replacements are being screened ever so carefully. Meanwhile, Noble Paperbacks is overinventoried with novels owed out on contract all over so why worry about it? *Next* year they'll get an editor.

It is possible by employing this fantasy to explain every defect in every science fiction novel published since, say, 1958 (when the magazine market collapsed and the magazines, through their somewhat more knowledgeable and rigorous editors, were the cutting edge of science fiction)—every truncated plot, rushed conclusion, unpredictable denouement, scientific error, sterile love scene, failed resolution. It is possible to understand all of it and to suggest that the few good novels of this era were not written on portion and outline, but this *is* a fantasy and may be disregarded. And by most of the readers (leave us not mention the writers) it certainly is.

Footnote to a fantasy: most of the important novels of the fifties originally appeared in the magazines whose editors commissioned them (like *Space Merchants* or *Demolished Man*) or worked them over pretty carefully (like *Dorsai!*). Most of science fiction's few acknowledged masterpieces in the novel appeared in the early to middle years of that decade. But then the distributors collapsed and so did plenty of magazine editors.

1980: New Jersey

Science Fiction and the Academy: Some Notes

According to late statistics compiled by the Science Fiction Research Association (SFRA), over a thousand colleges, junior colleges and universities throughout the land have courses devoted solely to science fiction. This is twice the number extant in the mid-seventies, almost ten times that of a decade ago and, when one considers that in 1960 there were perhaps two such courses in the United States (one of them taught at City College in New York on an adjunct basis by Sam Moskowitz), imposing. Part of this growth has to do with simple consumer economics: science fiction is something that they're reading, let's register them and grant credit to keep up the enrollment. (Most college catalogues are testimony to this philosophy of desperation.) Part has to do with the agonizingly slow but continuing legitimization of the field: some science fiction writers have broken through to critical recognition in other fields, and Leslie Fiedler did none of us any harm by declaring in the early seventies that he had always loved Phil Farmer (and now admired Norman Spinrad), but could not admit this until he became, at last, a tenured Distinguished Professor.

All of this is supposed to be good for science fiction, if not for science fiction *writers*, who are, with occasional exceptions, unable to teach courses for credit in their own field, made self-conscious by textual analyses and often photocopied and distributed without their knowledge or permission. The statement of the late sixties has already passed into the liturgy of the field (and has been claimed by a few): "It's time to get science fiction out of the academy and back in the gutter where it belongs." Analyzed out of existence, drained of mystery, codified to the final decree, science fiction, some of its writers fear, is on the way to becoming the Henry James or George Eliot of the twenty-first century.

Still, the academicization of the field, if only marginally helpful to the writers (and the students), can hardly be portrayed as an evil: it does not seem to have done much damage. The questions are a little more basic than those above but by their definition cannot be raised at the yearly conferences of the SFRA, the association of science-fiction-teaching college academics (two of which I have attended with great glee). They can however, be raised here, at least a couple of them.

The pervasive question is whether the field is *worth* teaching, whether there is sufficient text and insight to support a full-term college level course. Oddly, I heard this point raised not by a crusty Chaucer scholar, Dean of Student Affairs or member of the department of antiquities (in many places in many universities the academicization of "popular culture" is regarded as loathsome) but by one of the most experienced and sophisticated editors in the field, a credit to the genre to say nothing of a certified member of First Fandom. "What the hell is it?" he said, "a couple of lectures on the historical stuff, Wells and Verne and Chaucer and that crap which doesn't apply, has *nothing* to do with American science fiction and then the thirties and Heinlein and Campbell and when it got dirty in the sixties, but really, there just isn't that much to it. A few ideas, a few basic treatments and all of the variations; it's just a bunch of crap. Crap, crap," the editor mused and finished his whiskey sour and went onto other matters more pressing, although I cannot recall which.

A few writers, a few ideas, the same old variations? Not exactly, but the point is not superficial (nor is this editor a superficial man); is there enough about science fiction as distinguished from literature itself to justify it as a separate course unit, a heady three credits toward a baccalaureate? To the editor's point of view it would be as if a Bachelor of Music accepted in partial fulfillment a three-credit course on Khachaturian or the viole da gamba. Isn't it part of the continuing isolation of science fiction, another aspect of literary ghettoization, to render it a separate course within a Department of English (or Sociology) as something discrete, special, impenetrable? Why can't it simply be taught—for example, the works of Heinlein, Kuttner, Ballard, Kornbluth, Le Guin, Silverberg—as part of contemporary American literature?

Well, for once it might throw a lot of currently employed nontenured personnel out of work and reduce tuition input into the English Department. That is not a contemptible consideration. Then too, my perception at the SFWA conferences was, appositely, that instructors of science fiction were regarded by their academic colleagues almost exactly as editors of science fiction (even unto this day) are regarded by senior trade editors in the publishing houses. With few exceptions, the only way a science fiction editor can have a major editorial career* is to get out of science fiction and into something else (writers too). Anything will do for the shift. Science fiction academics, already functioning at the margins of their profession, will do anything to consolidate their position, and although a few might be able to move crosswise most will use their courses and enrollments to build up small power bases . . . which they hope to carry over to other universities should the need arise. There are very practical reasons why the SFRA catalogue a decade hence may double the number of colleges again; by 1990 *every* college and university in this country and most of the junior colleges as well may have a course in science fiction catalogued as routinely as Intermediate Algebra *first* . . . and will then seek someone to teach it.

What does it all mean? To appropriate my friend the edi-

---

* This has changed in the last few years . . . a major sf editor can be a major editor at some places now. But he has to stay in the field. Just like the writers, again.

tor's line, perhaps not very much. Some writers have expressed an amazing amount of (righteous) hostility toward this academicization because indeed the last person to teach science fiction in most of these places would be a science fiction writer. With tightening budgets and cuts in discretionary funding most courses now can administer their three credits without the students even *meeting*, for one session, a science fiction writer. Recrimination has always been the underside of these people; not inappropriately most science fiction writers have known in their hearts for years that they were generating a good deal of money for some people, very little of which ever got to them. The Harvards of the future perceived as the Bouregy Books of yesterday. Too—and although this is last it is in deference only to its simple truth—many of the academics are appallingly ill-informed. Their courses are superficial and filled with inaccuracies; they rarely diverge from the accepted canon, and they get much of that canon wrong. Students in many courses would be better informed had they been sent off to read a dozen books and Aldiss's *Billion-Year Spree* with the Nicholls Science Fiction Encyclopedia as backup.† The rendering of three academic credits for many of these courses is, if not an insult to the field (the field can take anything; it always has) then to the universities.

Ambivalence, then. Again. But somewhat less than expected: a hesitant vote after all for the academy. I was at one time quite hostile; credit Brian Aldiss for giving me the first quick turnaround of my life when, after I had mumbled some imprecations on a panel in 1975, he said, "No art can

† Since I might be asked then I might as well put it here to refer to forevermore—the science fiction reading list limited to that dozen books: *Adventures in Time and Space*, edited by Healy and McComas; *The Science Fiction Hall of Fame*, Volumes I, II, and IIA, edited by Silverberg and Bova; *The Arbor House Treasury of Modern Science Fiction*, edited by Greenberg and Silverberg; *The Astounding Science Fiction Anthology*, edited by John W. Campbell; *The Best of Science Fiction*, edited by Groff Conklin; *Again, Dangerous Visions*, edited by Harlan Ellison; *The Demolished Man*, by Alfred Bester; *More Than Human*, by Theodore Sturgeon; *A Canticle for Leibowitz*, by Walter M. Miller, Jr.; and *The Best of Damon Knight*.

be taken seriously without a body of criticism; the universities with all of their flaws are beginning to work us toward that body of criticism; we cannot reject them and aspire to be taken seriously."

"The man is right," I said on the instant. "The man is right and I am wrong. I see that now."

A year later, in different circumstances about a different matter, I said it again, not on a panel.

At the Divining Edge

Occasionally (less frequently all the time) I am called upon as the Town Science Fiction Writer (a role not dissimilar to that of Village Idiot) to speak to classes in the high school of my suburb in northeastern New Jersey. Genial in middle age and with my persona at reflex I can romp mindlessly through a fifteen-minute set piece on the joys and perils of the writing life, the custom of ambition and the habituation of form, and then throw the floor open to questions, which, after a grudging pause and a few glares from the English teacher, do come forth:

"What do you think of *Star Wars?* Do you think the sequel is better?"

"How about *Stranger in a Strange Land?*"

"Do you know Isaac Asimov? What is he really like?"

"The meaning of the end of *2001,* I never got it. What does it say? What do you think of *Planet of the Apes,* by the way?"

"Is Ray Bradbury any good?"

"Did you like *Star Trek: The Movie?*"

Well. Did I? Not sure. A little—ah—attenuated, I thought. Never saw the series, not ever, so can't compare. Bradbury? Ray Bradbury has appeared in a science fiction magazine exactly once in the last two decades and has not published a new story or book in ten years. I don't think too much of *Stranger in a Strange Land* (pretty good writer on balance, though) and haven't seen *The Empire Strikes Back* (loved the mysteriously truncated bar scene in *Star Wars,* though; why did they cut it so quickly?). The ending of *2001* is metaphysical or mystic, a dream of transcendence, and Asimov is a splendidly ebullient man, an example to us all. So what? (I would like to continue but do not.) Is that all that the general public, at least as represented in the high schools, thinks of science fiction? A couple of movies, a few writers, most of whom have published very little within the confines of the field since the 1950s? Doesn't anybody know or care what's really going on? The stylistic innovations of the last decade and a half, the enormous growth of audience for all kinds of science fiction, the ten to twenty modern science fiction writers who by any literary standard are first-rate? How about them, kids? Don't you care?

Someday, if I am invited back, I'll probably put these questions after all.

In the meantime, the questions resonate, which is a fancy, literary way of saying that they will not go away. Science fiction prospered in the 1970s; in a largely debased form it became big business for the media, but in a different fashion it also flourished as literature. There are in this country over a thousand people writing science fiction of publishable quality (a decade ago there were half that number), over twelve hundred books labeled "science fiction" were published in 1979 (again, it was half that number a decade ago), and one of our middle-range professionals can now expect an advance of $15,000–$20,000 for a novel that might have brought (and glad to have it) $5,000 in 1970. Silverberg's *Lord Valentine's Castle* received a $127,500 hardcover advance, Heinlein's *The Number of the Beast* over $500,000 for paperback; ten years ago the highest advance *ever* paid for a genre science fiction novel was $12,500 for the paperback rights to Silverberg's *The World Inside*. The level of ambition, the dazzling achievement of our best writers, the complexity and sophistication of a form that in the memory of some of its older writers like Williamson or Simak did not even *exist* when they began to write . . . quite wondrous. The universities will sort this out for a century.

But for the general public, the 95 percent whose reading is

of the most marginal level or less, science fiction is a couple of television series, a handful of films and four or five writers who were established well before 1950. Awareness of the category seems to be concentrated around a limited part of it: the rest of it is undiscovered.

This is depressing, but then so is the human condition. No particular reason to complain. How many high school students could name five living American novelists, three living serious composers? How many have even heard of, say, the *Hudson Review*, let alone have ever seen a copy? What percentage of that classroom has ever voluntarily gone to a symphony or a museum, opened *Ulysses* or *The Great Gatsby*? It is a hard time for us sensitive types in the so-called arts; if the students can name as many as five living science fiction writers they are, whether *I* like it or not, paying a kind of tribute to the field.

No, this is not what truly dismays. Rather it is a perception long after the fact; Buster Keaton would know how to do the take. I think that science fiction may be in severe trouble because not only the mass media but its best practitioners *themselves* have a clear interest in the category being known by and identified in the public consciousness with *Star Wars*, "Mork and Mindy," twenty-year-old novels by a couple of writers and all that stuff floating around the cabin in *Alien*.

Why this is so—or at least why I perceive it to be so—would make for a complex argument extended over many a wearying and wavering paragraph, but I will try to be concise:

Science fiction, from its inception as a subcategory of American literature in 1926, until very recently was a small and largely ignored pursuit for its readers and writers. It was regarded with contempt by the academic-literary nexus and ignored by the vast audience for popular culture. It had neither intellectual cachet nor, like television drama, the weight of attention.

This was unfair, to be sure, but it gave readers and writers (and editors and publishers too) the feeling that they were all collaborating on something vaguely disreputable, usually contemptible. When extrinsic events—Hiroshima, television, Sputnik, the assassinations, NASA, Apollo, "Star Trek," *Star Wars*—caught up to or seized the science fiction vision of transcendence, when those events *forced* the public to grudgingly accept the field as serious business after all, most of its creators were still caught by feelings of exclusion. The enormously successful science fiction of the last decades is known by serious followers to be poor, often dreadful, exemplification of the genre . . . but better popularity and acceptance than a return to the forties and fifties when it was impossible for anyone within the field to be taken seriously by anyone without.

So science fiction may eventually dominate the eighties on the basis of its worst or at least weaker possibilities.

Too bad. Too bad indeed. No proper focus for the anger, but I know the feeling . . . to dwell in a bad marriage . . . to sacrifice passion for the sake of peace . . . to sacrifice dignity in flight of pain.

1979/1980: New Jersey

Some Notes Toward the True
and the Terrible

I first made reference to the true and terrible unwritten history of science fiction in a review of James Gunn's *Alternate Worlds: The Illustrated History of Science Fiction* in 1975, but did not begin to develop the concept until I spoke at the University of California at Berkeley in 1978. Standing at the podium, shaking with fever, ampicillin, dread and wonder that any stranger would pay $3.75 cash on the barrelhead to listen to me,* I said that the history of science fiction must, by definition, exist truly in the interstices, that by definition the field could be explained only by material which would be by turns libelous, private, intuitive or paranoid and that even the most rigorous and lucid of scholarly works could deal only with symptomatic representations of the great underside of the field.

Surely I must have been anticipating that May the publication, a year and a half later, of the dense, scholarly and invaluable Encyclopedia of Science Fiction, edited by Peter Nicholls (the best reference work on our field which has appeared to date), because the Nicholls work manages through one intricate, brilliantly cross-referenced and almost impishly accurate volume to make clear to insiders and outsiders alike practically everything about science fiction that they would need to know to get through doctoral orals except for two factors: (a) How it got this way and (b) why it has its pecul-

* There were actually about forty such misguided souls in the audience, added to about 150 who had registered for a ten-session course called "The Writers Speak." Or mumble. Or drink. But never simultaneously if you want to be invited back.

iar and binding effect upon a readership, a larger proportion of which are emotionally involved with the literature than the readers of any other genre.

The Encyclopedia reminds me of the one-line criticism of Shaw's plays: that a literate alien could, from them alone, deduce everything about humanity except that it possessed genitals. Nicholls and his staff make everything about science fiction comprehensible except the existence of a 700,000-word trade paperback about it which can expect to sell eventually well over a million copies. Try that in quality lit, mystery or romance. The Gothic Encyclopedia? *The Illustrated History of Literary Writing? Barlow's Book of Flannery O'Connor?*

The true unwritten history is where the answers lie and the unwritten history cannot—by definition, be pointed out laboriously—be composed. In a spirit of scholarship and sacrifice, however, I would like to offer a few notes, leads as it were toward what it would contain and with what it would have to deal. Perhaps by the end of the twenty-first when all of us now reading, writing and propitiating the category are all safely dead and with the evolution of low-feed, multiplex stereophonic videotape cassette recall, the abolition of the written, that is to say, the true unwritten history might be retrieved.

To the unborn and penitent, hence, a few suggestions:

1) "Modern" science fiction, generally dated as having begun in late 1937 with the ascent of Campbell, was a literature centered around a compact group of people. It was no Bloomsbury but there could have been no more than fifty core figures who did 90 percent of the writing and the editing. All of them knew one another, most knew one another well, lived together, married one another, collaborated, bought each other's material, married each other's wives and so on. For a field which was conceptually based upon expansion, the smashing of barriers, the far-reaching and so on, science fiction was amazingly insular. One could fairly speculate that this insularity and parochialism were the understandable

attempts of frightened human beings faced with *terra incognita* to hold on to one another and to make their personal lives as limited and interconnected as possible. It could be speculated further that this parochialism shut off an entire alternative science fiction. (Alexei Panshin has intimated this possibility but not this particular set of reasons.) Who is to know what writers and manuscripts *not* connected in any way to the Central Fifty languished in slush piles or in stamped, self-addressed envelopes? Science fiction simply was not for them; it was being cooked up in offices and bars and bedrooms and apartment houses; people would stream from Central to write it all up in their own way and send it back in (and then write up next month's issue taking up the stuff already laid down in print), but the field was based on personal access and very few writers and stories were getting into the magazines without personal acquaintance with other writers and with the editors. The first thing that Damon Knight did in the forties as a science fiction writer *manqué* was to accept Fred Pohl's invitation to come out from Oregon to Brooklyn and live with the Futurian Club; the young Asimov was introduced to present contributors by Campbell before Asimov had sold a word; Malcolm Jameson, pensioned off by the Navy for medical reasons, began to write science fiction (and became, briefly, an *Astounding* regular in the mid-forties) at the urgings of his old friend and fellow Navy officer Robert A. Heinlein.

2) One of the clear symptoms of editorial decline (this ties, in a way, to the point above but only by suggestion; hear me out) is the increasing proportion of material in a magazine or book line written by a decreasing number of contributors; venery, laziness, exhaustion or friendship seem to make almost any long-term editorship vulnerable to this condition. (I am not saying that science fiction in this case is any different than any other genre.) The *Astounding* of the late nineteen-fifties had narrowed to four or five regular contributors in between whom a few asteroids squeezed the short

stories: Silverberg, Anvil, Garrett, Janifer/Harris and Reynolds must have accounted for 70 percent of the magazine's contents in the period 1958 to 1962. Over at *Galaxy* Fred Pohl, Robert Sheckley and Philip M. Klass must have contributed more than half the contents in the last three years of Horace Gold's editorship (1957–1960). This is not to dispute that this core group might have overtaken the magazines simply because they were the best, at least in terms of meeting the editorial vision (and there is no disputing that the *Galaxy* group at least includes three of the finest writers of science fiction thus far), but the consequences of such narrowing are obvious; the medium becomes insular and ambitious potential contributors become discouraged. There is, needless to say, a fine line an editor must tread between gathering the best writers he can and encouraging them . . . and buying from friends and familiars, but there is such a line of clear demarcation: Campbell in the early forties was on one side of it and in the late fifties on the other, and the quality of work and its persistence today (little of the late fifties *Astounding* is now reprinted) constitute judgement.

3) The clearest signal of Campbell's loosened grip and influence on the field from 1960 (the time at which his obsessive pursuit of pseudoscientific chicanery became his editorial obsession rather than weakness) is to compile a list of those writers who arose to prominence in that decade who never published in his magazine. Once for my amusement a long time ago (in the last couple of years of his life for I hoped that he would see it) I did so and published it in *Science Fiction Review*. Here is a partial (I am sure to miss someone) list of science fiction writers who did *not* appear in *Analog* from the issue of January 1960 until the last issue assembled by Campbell dated December 1971:

J. G. Ballard, Brian W. Aldiss, Ursula K. Le Guin, Samuel R. Delany, Joanna Russ, Larry Niven, Michael Moorcock, R. A. Lafferty, George Alec Effinger, Gardner R. Dozois, A. J. Budrys, Terry Carr, Kate Wilhelm, George Zebrowski, Norman Kagan, Theodore Sturgeon, Philip K. Dick, Pamela Sargent, Robert Sheckley, Roger Zelazny.

Silverberg *almost* makes the list; his last story was in the February 1960 issue (sold, of course, in the fifties). Tiptree's first story and one other appeared in *Analog*; Niven's first piece, published at last in 1972, was apparently Campbell's last purchase.

And yet. And yet when I heard of Campbell's sudden death on July 11, 1971, and informed Larry Janifer I trembled at Janifer's response and knew that it was so: "The field has lost its conscience, its center, the man for whom we were all writing. Now there's no one to get mad at us any more."

1980: New Jersey

Wrong Rabbit

And here is A. J. Budrys, who should know better in a fairly recent (May 1979) issue of *Fantasy and Science Fiction* discussing 1940s science fiction: "Modern science fiction as you know* was marked by a verve we do not often see these days, fueled by a pervading technological optimism and a set of ethical assumptions slightly to the right of the John Birch credo. Might was not only right, it was moral . . . technological action—exploring the physical possibilities and applying deft means of conveying maximum comfort to the maximum number of individuals—offers the best hope . . ."

It may do all of that—in the world which technology has bequeathed *only* technological action can accomplish change —but Budrys is wrong about the science fiction of Campbell's first decade, and before shibboleth passes all the way into law and the forties *ASF* is forever characterized as being packed by the Happy Engineer, I would like to, as the man said to the committee, try to set the record straight.

The Happy Engineer is one of the great uninvestigated myths of contemporary science fiction. (Another is that *Astounding/Analog* was/is devoted to stories whose background is "hard science" requiring "heavy tech," but that is *next* Sunday's text.) The truth, as any fresh confrontation of the material would certainly make clear, is that the forties *ASF* is filled with darkness, that the majority of its most successful and reprinted stories dealt with the bleakest implications of technology and that "modern" science fiction (defined by Budrys as that which originated with Campbell's editorship

* Say *what*, boss?

of *Astounding* given him in October 1937) rather than being a problem-solving literature was a literature of despair.

Only in the fifties as Campbell's vision locked and dystopia was encouraged by Horace Gold and Anthony Boucher did *Astounding* begin indeed to invite in the Happy Engineer: the complexities of Heinlein became the reflexive optimism of G. Harry Stine, Christopher Anvil, Eric Frank Russell (some of the time) and the somewhat more ambivalent optimism of Gordon R. Dickson, Poul Anderson or Randall Garrett. It would not be difficult to argue that this represented a drift from the *periphery* of the forties ASF: the *Venus Equilateral* stories of George O. Smith, say, or the *Bullard* series of Malcolm Jameson.

But consider the text entire. The Kuttners from the outset of their career were publishing stories of complexity and pessimism: "Mimsy Were the Borogoves" and "Shock" and "What You Need" and "When the Bough Breaks"† and the (superfically humorous) "Gallegher" series in which a drunken inventor's drunken inventions went crazy. "Jesting Pilot" and "Private Eye" and "The Prisoner in the Skull" were grim and desperate visions of the (failed) efforts to maintain autonomy and compassion in the shining, uncontrollable future. Heinlein's "Universe" is one of the grimmest visions in the history of the field; a centuries-long starflight gone astray, a civilization of the descendants of the original crew stripped of memory and reduced to barbarism.

Asimov's "Nightfall," not the best but certainly the best-known story Campbell ever published, describes the collapse of a civilization into anarchy and madness; L. Ron Hubbard's *Final Blackout*, a freehand template of World War II cast into an ambiguous future, depicts—as does Heinlein's *Sixth Column*—the use of the machineries of destruction to destroy linear cultural evolution. Heinlein's "By His Bootstraps" is a solipsistic nightmare cast as a time paradox story in which the protagonist cannot escape the simple and repeated loop of his life (and has for friendship only versions of himself). Van

† This giggler was about infanticide.

Vogt's work, from his first story "Black Destroyer" (a murderous alien loose on a spaceship kills most of the crew; the alien is in terrible emotional distress), put vision after horrid vision of the future into *ASF*, paranoid reaction toward militancy ("The Weapon Shops" series), the hopelessness of human evolution ("The Seesaw"), the collapse of causality (*The World/The Players of Null-A*).

In the wake of Hiroshima, Campbell published a series of apocalyptic stories (Kuttner's *Tommorow and Tomorrow & The Fairy Chessmen,* Chan Davis's "The Nightmare," Sturgeon's "Thunder and Roses") and postapocalyptic speculations (Russell's "Metamorphosite," Kuttner's "Fury") in such profusion that at the world science fiction convention of 1947, at which he was guest of honor, he begged for the fans' indulgence at the profusion of despair, claiming that he could only publish what the writers were delivering . . . but he *was* sending out pleas to cease and desist. (The writers got the message, finally, and fled to Gold and Boucher as soon as they opened shop.)

It could be said that by making good on this pledge, shutting down certain themes and approaches rather than (as before) encouraging the writers to get the best version of their ideas, Campbell was taking the first steps in the decline of his editorship and that the fifties *Astounding* can be seen as the product of a man who, having faced the abyss, had decided that he wanted no part of it. Through the fifties the other major editors accommodated the underside . . . but it must be noted that Godwin's "The Cold Equations," the best-known *ASF* story of the fifties, as "Nightfall" was the best-known of the forties, was a stunning and despairing enactment (a little girl stows away in a one-man rocket that does not have sufficient fuel to carry her and is jettisoned) of the limitations of technology, the implacability of the universal condition.

Seeing "modern" science fiction as cheerful and brave, upstanding and problem-solving—and Budrys is only the best of the critics to have taken this line; only John Clute seems to have disdained it thus far—makes for easy history of course: the primitive twenties, wondrous and colorful thirties, systematized and optimistic forties, quiet and despairing fifties, fragmented and chaotic sixties, expressionless seventies . . . and history, as has been noted, is an inherently comforting study, demonstrating, if nothing else, a retrospective order to what was chaotic. A proof that, at least, we got through.

But the price we are paying for this misapprehension is too high. It makes us consider science fiction as one thing when from the very beginning it surely was another.

Which makes us the inheritors of what we can never know, adopted children, scurrying obsessively through the closed or closing files of headquarters, seeking evidence that even if retrieved will be meaningless.

1980: New Jersey

John W. Campbell:
June 8, 1910 to July 11, 1971

Campbell. When I began to read science fiction in the fifties he *was* the field, an autocratic figure synonymous with the genre and as inaccessible to a twelve-year-old as—well, as Heinlein, Asimov or Duke Snider. I wrote him a couple of letters (I wrote the Duke a letter too) but received no reply (as with the Duke). Much later in the sixties when I started to write seriously in the field he was already the living symbol of everything that I had to overcome to make a contribution. Nonetheless, my early stories went to him first and the rejection slips became a personal repudiation, stoking my rage. In the seventies I won the first award given in his name and the cries of pain resonated in his magazine for months thereafter. Still resonate. The point seemed to be that *Beyond Apollo*, a despairing novel about the collapse into madness of the first Venus Expedition, was not exactly the kind of material Campbell would have published. Full of sex and dirty words too. An insult to his memory.

Everything that supersedes the dead must be an insult to their memory. The only real tribute—I know what I am talking about—would be for the world to end with them, and in a certain sense, with the large figures, it might. *Beyond Apollo* was, to me, a logical extension of John Campbell's editorial vision of the forties: if his magazine had continued to move past 1950 as it had in the previous decade, my novel would have fit almost indistinguishably into the pages of the 1972 *Analog*. Nonetheless, if there is no real tribute to the dead there is no arguing with them either; one can rave at them in the spaces of the night, prove one's father a fool, demonstrate to an uncle that it never could have worked his way after 1963 . . . but the dead have no comment, the arguments rebound to the damaged self, there is no answer, Lear, never, never, never, never, never. To accept the idea of one's death is at last to accept all the others and then after a long time the recrimination may end . . . but we never accept the idea of our own death, do we now, doctor? What do you think?

I have only one Campbell story but I think it is a fairly good one and worth entering in the ephemeral permanence of these pages; I told it for the first time in Chicago in April 1973 when accepting the Campbell award, but I don't think that anyone there got the point, least of all myself because it was many years later and in a different land before I understood, and now the wench is dead. (At least for me, alas. Generalizations are dangerous.) I met Campbell on June 18, 1969, a month and two days before the Apollo landing. As the newly installed volunteer editor of the *SFWA Bulletin* I had an excuse at last; I wanted to discuss "market trends," I said to him over the phone. "All right," he said, "same as ever though." What I intended to do, of course, was to finally, after two decades, meet the man who had changed my life. I knew the stories, the sacred texts and the apocrypha; I certainly knew what had happened to him since the fifties but intellection is not to feeling formed . . . regardless of my shaky professionalism I came to that desk with awe. Trying not to show it, of course. I was there to go the full fifteen or die. Float like a butterfly, sting like a bee. *I am the greatest/just you wait/Big John Campbell/Will fall in eight* I might have gibbered if I had had a Bundini.

I stayed with him in his office for three hours, fighting from the bell. Catherine Tarrant* sat at her desk in the far

---

* She was the only assistant Campbell ever had, joining him in 1938 and staying with the magazine until 1973. Catherine Tarrant died in Hoboken, New Jersey in March 1980, unnoticed and unmourned at the time (the obituary appeared in the sf publications months later) by anyone in the science fiction community. Campbell let it be known many times that in his mind she edited the magazine, he only chose the stories.

corner typing and making notes and trying hard not to smile. A young man's intensity can be a terrible thing to bear (for no one so much as the young man himself) and I came off the chair right away, throwing jabs, pumping and puffing, slipping the phantom punches, going in desperately under the real ones.

Not interested in market conditions, no sir. I wanted to know why *Analog* was the restrictive, right wing, antiliterary publication that it had become. Didn't Campbell care what all of the new writers, the purveyors of street fiction and venturesome prose, thought of him? "You've got to understand the human element here," the young man said, "it's not machinery, it's people, people being consumed at the heart of these machines, onrushing technology, the loss of individuality, the loss of control, *these* are the issues that are going to matter in science fiction for the next fifty years. It's got to explore the question of victimization."

"I'm not interested in victims," Campbell said, "I'm interested in heroes. I have to be; science fiction is a problem-solving medium, man is a curious animal who wants to know how things work and given enough time can find out."

"But not everyone is a hero. Not everyone can solve problems—"

"Those people aren't the stuff of science fiction," Campbell said. "If science fiction doesn't deal with success or the road to success then it isn't science fiction at all."

Much later—after his death—it occurred to me that he must have been lonely in those last years. Many things had changed in and out of science fiction in the late sixties, the writers were spread all over the country and didn't come up to the office much any more, the old guard had very little to do with him, the new writers were with Carr and Knight, Ellison and Ernsberger. Fred Pohl was responsible for buying the first stories of most of the writers who in the sixties were to go on to careers; Campbell's discoveries—he was still hospitable to unknowns—tended to stay in the magazine. If, like Norman Spinrad, they began to write a different kind of fiction and publish elsewhere, they were not welcomed back. At the time this seemed to be arrogance and editorial autocracy, but seen from Campbell's side it could only have been reaction to ingratitude and perversity. Why weren't *his* writers selling in the book markets and why did those who he broke in, so many of them, stop listening? It was very hard to handle and his sinusitis had turned to emphysema. Gout made him limp. Some fanzines were venomous.

"Mainstream literature is about failure," Campbell said, "a literature of defeat. Science fiction is challenge and discovery. We're going to land on the moon in a month and it was science fiction which made all of that possible." His face was alight. "Isn't it wonderful?" he said. "Thank God I'm going to live to see it." (He must have been thinking of Willy Ley, who had died just a few weeks before. Ley, the science columnist of *Galaxy*, had been with the German Rocketry Society in the thirties, had dedicated his working life to the vision of space travel. The timing of his death was cruel; even though they had been at odds for almost twenty years Campbell had gone to the funeral and been shattered.)

"The moon landing isn't science fiction. It comes from technological advance—"

"There's going to be a moon landing because of science fiction," Campbell said. "There's no argument."

Probably there wasn't. (Most of the engineers and scientists on Apollo had credited their early interest in science to the reading of science fiction, which meant, for almost all of them, *Astounding*.) Still, the young man's intensity had turned at last to wrath. Here was the living archetype of science fiction, right here, and he wasn't reasonable.

No, he was just a stubborn, close-minded, bigoted sixty-year-old who had endorsed Wallace in 1968, had said that the Chicago police hadn't hit long or hard enough and was now pursuing dowsing as a legitimate research method. I lunged at him verbally. Engaged he lunged back. We argued civilization. The electoral process (Campbell thought most were too dumb to deserve the vote). The fall of cities, the collapse of postindustrial democracy because of the pervading effect of ideologies like Campbell's. ("Good," Campbell said, "we'll find something better.") The editor would not budge. Neither would the soon-to-be-editor emeritus of the *SFWA Bulletin*. It became, at great length, one o'clock. The young man twitched like an elongated White Rabbit. "Better go," he said, "better go, it's late. I'm late." For nothing. But I would not presume on Campbell's time further. Besides, it was time for his lunch. Besides, arguing with him had made me sick.

"All right," Campbell said. Much later too I realized that he might have wanted me to go out with him, but in light of the argument knew no way to ask. "Nice talking to you."

"Nice talking to *you*," I said. "An honor." I stood shakily, took his hand, shook it, nodded at Catherine Tarrant and stumbled down the corridor. Later I stood by the elevator bank at 420 Lexington Avenue and waited.

For quite a long time. While I stood there, briefcase clutched, trying to straighten my tie with one hand (I was a self-important young fella) the fuller sense of the morning came over me. The schism between us, the irreparable distance, the sheer unreason of this man from whom I had learned so much, expected so much more. There were, if you considered it in one way, aspects of tragedy here.

It should not have come to this; it was terribly sad. I began to shake with recrimination. It was wrong. This was not the way Campbell should have ended, the way it should have been the only time I met him—

Still no elevator.

Around a corner loomed suddenly the figure of John Campbell on his way either to or from—I surmised—the lavatory. He regarded me for a while. I looked back at him, shook my head, sighed, felt myself shaking as a sound of despair oinked out.

A twinkle came into the Campbell eye as he surveyed it all.

"Don't worry about it, son," he said judiciously. And kindly after a little pause. "I just like to shake 'em up."

So he did.

And so do I try. Still.

1980: *New Jersey*

The Science Fiction
of Science Fiction

Robert Silverberg's two 1970s stories, "The Science Fiction Hall of Fame" (1972) and "Schwartz Between the Galaxies" (1973) are central to any analysis of the form; they are extremely important as works of literary criticism and may in that regard transcend their value as fiction (which is not to say that as fiction they are contemptible). Neither has received a great deal of attention; short stories in this category rarely do. Neither in my opinion has been properly understood, because to properly grasp these stories is, perhaps, to cease reading and writing science fiction. It is astonishing, a tribute to professionalism and the contradictory nature of the writers' persona that Silverberg continued to write past these stories, and after a three-year pause seems to stand on the verge of yet another major career, his third in this field.

(But this is not to single out Silverberg. My own 1973 *Herovit's World* reads like the last will and testament of a bitterly exhausted writer about to quit science fiction; that posture *did* become mine for a time but only three years later. Between *Herovit's World* and my public scream of pain I wrote more than fifteen additional science fiction novels and a hundred short stories. Persistence or the beckonings of the market, culture lag or most likely of all proof of Robert Sheckley's aphorism: It is very hard to learn from something that we already know.)

To jump the argument herein right to the end and to anticipate my conclusion (a habit quite common among writers who fear the point may otherwise wriggle off like a fish and evade them forever), what Silverberg is clearly saying in both "Schwartz" and "The Science Fiction Hall of Fame" is that science fiction is doomed by its own nature and devices to be a second-rate form of literature. It can *never* aspire to the effects of the first rate which are to break the reader (and writer) through to new levels of perception, to a reorganization of the materials of his life. It cannot do this because the purposes of science fiction, at the base, must work against this kind of heightening of insight, confrontation of self.

Yet at the same time that both of these stories drive through to the point conclusively, they are *themselves* very close to first-rate work. "The Science Fiction Hall of Fame" is not science fiction (it is a literary story which incorporates the genre as a metaphor for the protagonist-narrator's condition), but "Schwartz Between the Galaxies" *is,* and the fact that the latter at least can take the reader to a conclusion which the existence of the story denies is one of those large or little paradoxes not uncharacteristic of the field. The tension between what is said and what is meant—what is indicated and what is done. It is all of a mystery.

"The Science Fiction Hall of Fame" was published in *Infinity Three,* a long-departed volume of an extinct original anthology series (it reached five volumes; a sixth was compiled but never published) edited by Robert Hoskins. It is less a work of fiction than what the French might call a meditation: the nameless protagonist, employed in an unstated executive job in an anonymous corporation, discusses the role that his obsession with reading and collecting science fiction has imposed upon him. He is ambivalent about science fiction: on the one hand he feels that it is a carryover of adolescent escapism and fantasizing which, shamefully, he has not been able to put away; on the other he feels that the transcendent and predictive qualities of the genre grant him broader perspective than most of his friends in the corporate lower middle class. (But he feels vaguely embarrassed defending the genre to his friends and conceals his library.) He fornicates with a lady friend while watching the Apollo landing;

the moment of orgasm, colliding with the first steps on the moon (a coincidence which would not work with ninety writers out of a hundred but which Silverberg makes appealing through dry understatement), yields only a sense of blankness, the same blankness which he feels at this culmination of the science-fictional vision. Old magazine covers and paragraphs from the classic stories drift through the protagonist's mind toward sleep; he can chant the names of the greats and of their oeuvre. The story comes to no conclusion whatsoever but it is fair to say that if it had appeared in *The New Yorker* (where it would have fit in stylistically without a tremor) instead of *Infinity* it would have been taken as a perfectly turned template of late-century urban angst and loss as portrayed through the metaphor of escapist fiction. The story, one of Silverberg's finest, has attracted virtually no attention, probably because it is not science fiction and its true audience (whatever that audience might be) has never found it.

"Schwartz" has attracted some attention and *is* science fiction; it appeared in the first issue of the Judy-Lynn del Rey occasional original anthology, *Stellar Science Fiction*, and was until late 1980 (when "Our Lady of the Stegosaurs" appeared in *Omni*, to be followed by several others) Silverberg's apparent last short story. Schwartz, a 22nd-century physicist with psychological and emotional problems of minor crippling nature, is a science fiction fan; on a star flight he sinks further and further into the fantasies of pulp magazines while the technologized, metallic present recedes; barely able to cope with his environment Schwartz appears to sink toward clinical depression as the rocket approaches its destination and not a moment too soon.

Silverberg is reiterating the vision of "The Science Fiction Hall of Fame" but with less ambivalence here, possibly with less moral complexity;* here is the speculation, quite naked, that science fiction in *any* era will be a junk medium. The sci-

---

* I say this because Schwartz is so clearly a loser; the narrator of "The Science Fiction Hall of Fame" is in conventional societal terms at least holding his own.

ence fiction of the science fiction future will partake then as ever of the elements of fantasy and escape, will serve the readers' need for the dreamlike, will shift him (with his active collaboration) off reality.

The very purposes of science fiction in short must render it contemptible in absolute literary (or psychological) terms. Literature deals with life, the story would suggest; science fiction sends us messages of its warpage or denial. Schwartz tumbling through the black holes of the ninth millennium would yet meander through pulp imaginings, dreaming perhaps of brave astronauts making moon landings or inventing holographic television transmitters.

Like "Science Fiction Hall of Fame," "Schwartz" is therefore less a work of fiction than of literary criticism. (Silverberg has stated that he thinks it is one of his five best; I think that a reasonably close reader would not take it that high, but it is close and detailed work and both better conceived and adventurous, if not as emotionally affecting, as "Science Fiction Hall of Fame.") It is, in fact, a castigation of the genre which perpetrated it and in which it appears, and as such it is devastating, a demolition of the genre so compelling that one surmises that if Judy-Lynn del Rey had truly understood what Silverberg was saying she would have refused to publish the story. (This may be too harsh; Silverberg recounts that del Rey was not too happy with it on delivery, calling it something that she had not expected, but it would be more than possible for her to publish it as a politic gesture to a major career without having much use for it at all.) Certainly it is easy to see why it was Silverberg's last short story for seven years and why after two more relatively unambitious novels (*The Stochastic Man* and *Shadrach in the Furnace*) Silverberg backed away from science fiction for several years. There is no place a serious science fiction writer can go from "Schwartz" other than to consciously cut back on the range and implication of the material. ("Lord Valentine's Castle" and "Our Lady of the Stegosaurs," published at the time of this writing, clearly indicate that this is, for now at least, so.)

"Schwartz" and "Science Fiction Hall of Fame" (along with a few of my own works, particularly *Herovit's World* and *Galaxies*) are close to the final position statement but they have interesting antecedent in Samuel R. Delany's well-known "Aye, and Gomorrah," which appeared in *Dangerous Visions* in 1967 and won a Nebula Award; Delany tosses away in subtext what Silverberg brought up front but the clues are there. In his story the science fiction of today has become the cheap adventure fiction of the century following and is read (among others) by perverts who are sexually aroused by (desexualized) astronauts: science fiction has become tomorrow's pornography. In one shattering throwaway description of the cheap magazines and paperbacks kept by one of the frelks (astronaut-lovers) in his apartment Delany opened a crack on Silverberg's devastating insight: Science fiction is junk. Junk by definition misrepresents, lies, cheapens, manipulates—junk may even be said to destroy (but only if one is already open to destruction), but ultimately junk can serve only the debased purposes of those who consume it: they are not seeking enlightenment but comfort. Delany has other, and perhaps less profound, matters on his mind in this story but he foreshadows what Silverberg in the best tradition was able to explore at greater length many years later.

(Any discussion of this subgenre's subgenre must fairly make reference as well to the late Edmond Hamilton's 1964 *Fantasy and Science Fiction* story, "The Pro," in which an old pulp science fiction writer, father of an astronaut, returns from a view of the launching to look at the dead colored magazines and books on his shelf, "lined up like little paper corpses," and understands that not only in relation to his son's career but to all of life his work has meant absolutely nothing, has borne no relation to any reality except the brief purposes to which his fiction was conceived and published, now of no value whatsoever. He could not get the curious reporters, looking for a human interest angle, to understand that and he could barely accept it himself but now, as The

Pro stares at the collected and forgotten works, the tears come. The story was reprinted only once in *The Best of Edmond Hamilton* and this paragraph is, to my knowledge, the first printed notice it has ever received. Hamilton died in early 1977 at the age of seventy-three. All of his work is now out of print. Much of *Star Wars* and *The Empire Strikes Back* appear to be based upon a close reading of his work. At least his wife, Leigh Brackett, who herself died only a year later, was commissioned to do the original script for *The Empire Strikes Back*.)

What does all of this mean? What is the question? as Gertrude Stein is reputed to have finally said. The Silverberg stories—and Delany's and Hamilton's too in a different way—lead to brooding if not awfully complex speculation on the nature of the field to which I have dedicated a large proportion of my working life and most of my best creative energies. And two and a half million words of fiction. The questions are by their nature irresolute but at least they can be posed, no small step for a middle-aged genre writer. Is science fiction doomed indeed to be a second-rate literature? Does its very nature demand that?

Or is this too bleak? Might the genre be shaped or at least left open to the possibility that it could lead toward an explanation of the better rather than worse possibilities? Might science fiction become, somehow, not a literature of escape but (as Alexei Panshin has suggested) one of education for survival? Might science fiction, in short, somehow be worked around as the Futurians of the late thirties were sure it could be, to *save the world?*

Science fiction to save the world is a catechism which predates even the Futurians. The earliest practitioners of the form as defined by Gernsback believed by the early thirties in nothing less. The history of organized fandom according to the concordance of Moskowitz (footnotes by Harry Warner, Jr.) can be understood as the history of a group splitting early between those who loved science fiction for its own sake and those who saw it as a political-social instrument of change;

the schism became ugly, and even uglier were some of the effects of the decades on those who believed that it *could* matter. As late as the nineteen-fifties, most of the field's best writers—Kornbluth, Clifton, Budrys, Heinlein—and certainly almost all of its important editors, believed that the literature had the power within itself to change society, to genuinely alter institutions and personal lives. (Hubbard's Dianetics, an invention which emerged wholly from science fiction, was an attempt to codify the personality and therapy in terms which could have been those of *Astounding*'s engineer-readers; perform the proper rituals and remove the engram, schematize the psyche and quantify the Bad Charge.)

Most science fiction writers no longer believe this. Some do but have resorted to mystical rather than practical rationalization. Panshin in his nineteen-seventies critical works *Farewell to Yesterday's Tomorrow* and *SF in Dimension* posits a science fiction which will deliver universe, possibility and transcendence. Robert Heinlein's most recent enormous novels use the devices of science fiction as mystical extrapolation. (*Stranger in a Strange Land*, the first and best of them, found an enormous audience, a few of whom did not interpret Heinlein's vision in exactly that way.) There is to this time a strong undercurrent in science fiction toward the use of the genre as a positive, engaging, didactic, *useful* medium for its readers. Science fiction as self-improvement; a kind of complicated Couéism for the last quarter of the century. *Getting better with science fiction*; Valentine Smith as another version of Bruce Barton's Jesus who, whatever else He might have been, was surely one of the boys. And a hell of a salesman.

But "Schwartz" and "The Science Fiction Hall of Fame" will simply not go away. Once read—and anyone who would consider himself a student of this genre will eventually read them—they render a statement which must be taken into account. Science fiction will *always* offer easier alternatives. Science fiction will *always* be slanted, by definition, to taking its readers out of the world. Only weak people, however—pat

Freudianism and the great cult psychology movements of the seventies have taught us—want out of the world. Strong people want *in*. Strong people want to, must deal with life as it is presented. Science fiction is a literature for the weak, the defenseless, the handicapped and the scorned. Panacea and pap.

I have presented the poles of the argument. I have no conclusion. Here is the ambivalence locked not only into the field but in me (and perhaps, although I hesitate to generalize, in every writer who ever attempted to do a serious body of work in science fiction or even took it seriously enough to start). It would be nice to conclude positively, satisfying a large portion of the readership; it would be satisfying to end negatively if only to carry through the integrity of one's vision, but I can do neither. I have no answer nor can I even recommend where it may be sought. Science fiction is an ambivalent genre.

It is an ambivalent genre and I have been, perhaps, its most ambivalent writer. The career and Collected Works, the life itself, have been monument or mausoleum to schism. The field is one thing and yet it may be the other. I am one thing and yet the other. I, the field, may be both but somehow I doubt it. One cannot embrace multitudes; one can barely (and only then if life is lived well) embrace oneself. There is simply no conclusion.

This genre, this thing, this science fiction, may make us better, it may make us worse. It may make us anything and then again, *pace* Hamilton, it may make us nothing at all, be entirely useless, a bunch of futuristic or bizarre stories. That's all folks, take them or leave them as you will, and most of you will leave them. It is everything and nothing, better and worse. It is intolerably—and finally—merely human.

And that is what drew me toward it. A path not of illumination but of thrall. To become at last what one beholds— and dare not know the difference.

I Don't Want Her
You Can Have Her—

The fans with their acronyms have the name for it all right: GAFIATE, *getting away from it all*. In the active form, to gafiate. The reaction is well known. Exhaustion, loathing and overwhelming futility attack the actifan. Enmeshed in a hardly seamless network of conventions, fanzines, correspondence, feuds, history and obligation he feels a poetic faintness. He ceases to respond to letters; he is seen at conventions no more. Feuds and lovers must find other objects. The fan has gafiated. Sometimes he makes an announcement to this effect. More often—gafiation by definition is silence— he allows inferences. He returns to school full time. He gets married out of the field or files for divorce within it. He runs for congress or becomes employed by a distinguished graduate division.

Sometimes the gafiation is permanent (there are figures who will not even *admit* their participation in fan activity; will rip up the texts of Warner or Moskowitz undetected in bookstores). Quite often it is not. The fan, after a period of recuperation, degafiates. Once again he is seen at conventions, begins to query contributors for his reborn fanzine. APAs bristle with fresh reminiscence. Of course, in another few months or years the revulsion like malaria may set in once more: once more the pain. There are people whose lives can be defined in terms of successive involvement and flight from organized science fiction.

The same thing happens to writers and, for that matter, casual readers. The writer will deal with science fiction no more. He cannot write power fantasies for a juvenile audience, he is restricted by the editors, enchained by taboo, he will seek a wider audience and artistic freedom in the mainstream. Suitable announcements are made. The casual reader —for that matter, the *heavy* reader—has lost a sense of wonder. Eyes glaze, sensibility clouds; science fiction, like the booze in the second act of *The Iceman Cometh*, no longer has that old kick. He will read real novels about real people. The reader and writer turn their energies to another focus— the reader, usually adolescent, at first gafiation begins to entertain a social life—but they will be back. You can count on it. Unless, of course, they are not. Permanent gafiates appear to be the rule in only one class, those who in early adolescence, for a brief period of time, read great quantities of science fiction in a brief lacuna between childhood and the onset of a purposeful sex drive. (Decades later these people will not even *remember* reading science fiction in quantity and they will not be lying or self-deluded—science fiction was indeed an extension of a persona that the glands' development demolished.) All of the others, in one fashion or the other, are heard from again. They can be said to have ungafiated and the terminology and the literature have categorized that syndrome as well.

This central ambivalence in the science fiction reader and writer—an ambivalence not common among those involved in any other kind of literature although quite familiar (in other areas) to students of abnormal psychology or those involved with the great religious institutions—is perhaps the central fact of the category, the lever to mix a metaphor into any profound understanding of this dark and troubled literature. The ambivalence comes from the conflicting perceptions of the form: Is it a true literature of the future, a forward-looking, transcendent, mind-boggling, mind-stretching form which renders its readers superior to the population, or is it just a bunch of crazy power fantasies and speculations (admittedly some of them better written than others) for the sublimation of powerless adolescents? Is it a literature whose roots are contemptible or exalting? Every one of us has felt strongly in one way and then the other through the course of our involvement and very few of us have managed to resolve the schism. Gafiation is an expression of one perception when pushed to the extreme but gafiation may itself be an act of collaboration . . . one has taken science fiction seriously enough, been moved by it to sufficient degree to need to put an official imprimatur upon one's rejection. Surely the millions who have read one or two science fiction stories, have not liked them particularly and have not looked at science fiction since have not gafiated. They were never in a circumstance from which they could gafiate at all.

The ambivalence is not only at the center of everyone's relationship to the form but probably at the center of the genre itself. Almost all of our strong works—and a good many of the weaker ones in the bargain—have derived much of their power from the evident struggles of the writers to fuse elaborate and often bizarre speculation with character and situation which will give the speculation emotional force. "The disparate and technological, the desperate and human," Samuel R. Delany said many years ago, this is the definition of science fiction. The desperate and the disparate, the technological and the human do not link up easily; however, the fusion can be made—*Rogue Moon, A Canticle for Leibowitz,* Delany's own "Aye, and Gomorrah," to which his remarks were afterword, indicate that it can be done—but the psychic costs for writers and readers are severe. It is, after all, what started out as a crazy literature about aliens and robots, rocket ships and planetary destruction; it was deliberately published in the most debased form and slanted to appeal to a juvenile audience. As the consequence of the decades and of the perversity of its writers and editors, the pain and implication began to be put in . . . but there is a point at which even an excellent writer, a sophisticated reader begins to question the very nature of the material to which he is devoting so much time and thought. Surely there must be a better occupation for a grown human being than to define the world in deliberately removed form. It is better to deal with the world directly. Have an affair, get a degree in computer science, write a historical novel about events which *did* occur.

Spend some time with the kids, sell off the magazine collection.

Hence, gafiation. But there is nothing approaching a real cure for the seriously afflicted; one may amputate the limb but must henceforth live in apprehension of its loss, limp around. Sometimes it is simply easier to accept one's condition, go back to it. Up to a point of course. And then at a lower level, satiation is reached once again and one begins to toy with the idea of gafiation, which the second or third time is hardly such a major step. After all, one has *already* lived through it. . . .

There is really no solution to any of this; science fiction, as Delany hints, is the literature of irresolution. Its readers and writers will inevitably feel pulled out at some point and some will feel that way always even though few can forsake it utterly. No creators or audience for any branch of popular entertainment love and hate their form as do those involved in science fiction. (There is almost no organized fandom for westerns and mysteries; quality lit fandom is oxymoronic and there are no situation comedy conventions. There are soap opera fan luncheons and comics conventions but they appear to be commerce, not seduction.) No creators or audience hate and love one another as do science fiction people. No creators or audience can be said to hate or love *themselves* as do——

Why? Because it is a crazy escapist literature and yet contains the central truth of this slaughterhouse of a century. We know this and cannot at times bear the thought of it. Nor, considering the record of the century and the horrors which the millennium hurtles toward us, is there reason why we should.

But one cannot—except in a few dramatic and pitiful instances in science fiction—voluntarily gafiate from the century.

1980: New Jersey

Onward and Upward With the Arts
Part II

Even a modestly successful science fiction writer—say, a
dozen short stories in the magazines and a paperback original
—can get on the convention circuit, and some of them never
get out. There is in this land at least one science fiction convention every weekend of the year (excepting perhaps Christmas and New Year's), and on many weekends the aspirant
has his choice of two or three. The conventions take place in
large cities and small, they range in attendance from one hundred or less* to seven thousand,† some are longstanding and
traditional (the world convention is approaching the end of
its fourth decade, the Cincinnati convention its third); others
are fly-by-nights or just beginning to build. One some years
ago took place on trains which racketed back and forth between Washington and New York while fans trooped lively
through the corridors. It is difficult to speculate the effect on
nonconventioneers. (The train was not a charter.)

The conventions are of all size and location but the pro-
grams are much the same. Fans attend, as do casual readers
who live in the area (depending upon the degree of publicity), and editors and writers and, of course, the press. There
are panels on all aspects of the field, a guest of honor who
delivers a guest-of-honor speech, discussion groups, movies,
meet-the-pros parties. (At larger conventions many of these
events occur simultaneously.) There is a costume party, a
grand masquerade. Private parties are held through the prem-

* Hexacon, Lancaster, Pennsylvania.
† The 1980 World Science Fiction Convention in Boston.

ises celebrating various regions, interests or friendships and sometimes celebrating nothing at all. The hotel bar is filled with professionals and their editors. (Fans themselves, because of age and disposition, tend to be a nondrinking crowd.) There is a good deal of fornication, not all of it indiscriminate. Old rivalries and hatreds are renewed, reworked or broadened. Although the faces of the fans may change from region to region, those of the writers, editors and the *serious* fans do not: Denver is very much like Minneapolis; Boston is Cincinnati *redux*.

Science fiction—as I have written elsewhere in a different voice a long time ago—for all of its claims to being a mind-expanding, venturesome field is much like the dog show circuit, the same handlers and judges appearing in different combinations everywhere. The world of the convention like the world of Nabokov's *Lolita* is an endless series of rooms in different places, all of which look the same. Only through the souvenir shops could one tell the difference.

For a new writer—and many an older one—it is all very heady stuff indeed. There are panels, autographs to be signed, nametags to display, new fornicatrices or drinking partners to be gained; the winds of Seattle's heath may howl, the gales of Philadelphia may blow, but inside the hotel it is comfortable and familiar and it is unnecessary to go out at all. Most attendees do not; always one plans to sightsee but things keep on getting in the way. A science fiction writer who, like all American writers but five or six, lives in anonymity and discontent, can find at the conventions what no other writer outside the province can: recognition and an audience. The panels are attended, the guest-of-honor speeches are heard, the books are there to be autographed and every smile is a winner. It is possible for the duration of a convention—and beyond—to believe that science fiction is the world.

It is not, of course, and in his heart the professional probably knows this, but that requires thought, and conventions work against the activity. Of the 500,000 who can be said to read as many as three science fiction books a year (this already less than a quarter of a percent of the population), only a tenth of them could be identified as serious, devoted readers, and perhaps a fifth of that tenth, or 10,000, compose that pool from which *all*‡ convention attendees can be said to be drawn. The total convention-going population would at the best fail to fill Madison Square Garden. Early season with the Warriors in town.

Still, at the large conventions they all seem to be there, including many beautiful women (there were almost no women at conventions until the nineteen-sixties). The drinks flow, the professionals hang out in a community of misery, the speeches draw applause and there is always the possibility that the next request for an autograph may bring a "serious relationship." Editors are always impressed by writers receiving adulation, so there is no mystery to science fiction writers getting on the circuit—all have been powerfully tempted; the circuit is also the reason why so many promising careers have hung at promise for years, or collapsed; still the illusion of audience is better for a writer (and more pleasant by far) than the anonymous, grinding work which is the lot of the commercial fictioneer. It is possible to combine the two—grinding work, weekend conventions—but this can bring real burnout; only a few remarkable cases have been able to work them together, and one will never know the price extracted from celebrated livers and bowels.

The existence of the circuit is probably the central reason for a well-known phenomenon: science fiction is an art medium in which one can go from quite promising to washed up without having paused for even a day at a point between. But the last word should be that of an ex-science fictioneer (who fled both the field and the circuit a long time ago) who

‡ This was a perfect summation of the situation just prior to the early seventies; now a good proportion of convention attendees are not readers at all but have been funneled in by "Star Trek," *Star Wars* and so on. Whether this is better or worse is for the writer to figure out; it's every man for himself in this game.

said, "You know, you can get a great deal of attention, real reverence at these conventions for sure. But you know when the trouble begins? It starts when you ask who in hell you're getting this attention *from.*"

1980: New Jersey

Tell Me Doctor If You Can
That It's Not All Happening Again

Replication is the stuff of marriage, middle age and science fiction; the portents are heavy and the air is foul. In late 1959—as in late 1937 on a less cosmic scale—the market for science fiction was in a state of collapse. The magazines, the deaths, the distributors, the book publishers. A well-known American fan and editor, Earl Kemp, passed around the Detroit World Science Fiction Convention with a questionnaire asking responses to the question, *Who killed science fiction?* and he had enough speculations and rumblings to publish a *book* (which won an unprecedented Hugo Award in the fan magazine category a couple of years later). Dismal clumps of editors and writers gathered in bars and bedrooms to ask one another whether the field could even be said to exist anymore. There was one fairly viable magazine (*Astounding*), a couple of others obviously in distress, and a scattering of paperback book publishers, none of whom expressed much interest in paying more than small advances to writers whose work they had already published. Detroit was a terrible time; a convention which lives on in the memory of the assembled as surely postfuneral but without even the wistful gaiety of the wake.*

Many of Earl Kemp's respondents confessed their feeling that science fiction had indeed been murdered, that its existence as an independent, functioning subgenre of American literature had reached its end just as had the sports pulp, the

* Detroit and Chicago were competing bidders in 1980 for the 1982 world convention; no fools they—the fans went for Chicago. Or perhaps, fandom being self-renewing and ahistorical, the current bunch simply *liked* Chicago.

air war stories, combat fiction, jungle stories and the like. (In the great pulp era of the nineteen-thirties there had been several magazines devoted to such arcana as railroad fiction or espionage. The war and paper shortages had put an end to almost all of these magazines and television in the postwar era guaranteed that they would never be revived; truly almost all of the pulp era readers seemed to prefer television, and readers who would have come into the market after the war, of course, had no choice.) To this time, those science fiction writers who were active at the end of the era are able to talk of the late nineteen-fifties only with loathing. Most of them gave up their careers—by choice, circumstance or a fortuitous blending of the two—and most of them never returned. The markets revived but this generation of writers was gone.

More than two decades later we know that American science fiction was not murdered. It had a whopper of a heart attack, it lay in the intensive care ward for quite a while (and had like most indigents to somehow find its way to the hospital itself), but time and a little fresh air did wonders for the patient who toddled out of the hospital in 1965 and has not yet returned (although there have been little murmurs and seizures, flutters of panic). Over a thousand titles labeled "science fiction" have been published every year since 1978, no less than fifty writers can be said to be making a substantial-to-extravagant living through the writing of science fiction alone, and although the magazines have been pushed steadily to the borders of the market—only *Analog, Amazing* and *Fantasy and Science Fiction* survive from the fifties; only *Isaac Asimov's* and *Omni* have persisted from their birth in the late seventies to join them, though *Omni* publishes very little fiction—the science fiction short story lives on in the original anthology form and is the basis for many expansions to novel length. The science fiction novel has become the most reliable single category in American mass-market publishing; 15 percent of all fiction titles published are now science fiction, and most of these books are at least marginally profitable for their publisher.

Nonetheless, the dystopian undercurrent flows in science fiction; it has from the genre's inception. (Letters in the *Astounding* of the mid-thirties were already asking where all the good stuff had gone; correspondents to *Astounding* in the late forties were expressing the hope that with the war over Campbell could now get some of the decent kind of fiction that he had been publishing before Pearl Harbor.) Perhaps it has to do with the psychic defensiveness of the science fiction reader, but it also is based upon extrinsic and verifiable realities. The writers, the more experienced editors and the older-generation fans often wake up screaming, in minor versions of the combat flashback syndrome, from dreams that it has all happened again. "*Is* it happening again?" they ask themselves, and not only in their individual cubicles of the night. Every retrenchment in a publisher's line, every transfer of a magazine ownership, every significant editor fired brings up the question: *the late fifties again?* Regardless of the changes in the field, expansion of at least the fringe audience, security of backlist and the essentially benign commercial history of the last decade . . . is science fiction due nonetheless for another collapse?

The cyclical history of the field, the omens and the portents might so indicate, but science fiction writers and readers are supposed to be rationalists, and some factors which applied in 1959 do not apply now. It is no longer a magazine medium hooked to the whims of distributors and a transient audience but instead is tied into the media by conglomerate ownership and by the fact that the most successful movies of recent years—*Star Wars*, *The Empire Strikes Back*, *Alien*—have all been science fiction and have funneled new readers steadily into the field. (Most of them, alas, dropping out soon.) We all like to think too that we are older and wiser, that like Anouilh's priest in *The Lark* we have seen it all before and thus do not need to see it again. The most powerful delusion of a career in the writing of any fiction is that one's work grows and improves, that things need ultimately not be the same but in changing will get better . . . that there is a difference.

Still, even with the safeguards and delusions, not unlike those "safeguards" and "brakes" which economists remind us over and over again in their newspaper columns make a recurrence of the depression impossible, one cannot really be sure. There are no certainties in show biz. Conglomerate publishing can be merciless to a losing proposition (the same people who kill television series after two episodes or refuse to proceed with a pilot in the face of negative advertiser reaction are now the people who ultimately control publishing), producing fear among the writers and editors alike. At a recent world convention† the editors were on short expense accounts and mostly in hiding; the writers entertained one another with tales of editorial treachery and incompetence, publisher stupidity and retrenchment.

Make this point: what most readers of science fiction do not know and have little reason to suspect is the degree to which the very quality of fear can be said to control the acquisition, production, marketing and selling of science fiction in this country and how all of these subsidiary fears refract back to the first, that of the writer trying to survive by the medium who, professionally, must engage in self-censorship, must understand that there are certain stories he cannot write. The writer—the experienced writer in any event—knows that most editors acquire and publish not in an effort to be successful so much as to avoid failure.‡ Defensive driving. They seek, then, that which they consider safe, and the writers who are at the mercy of these editors* function from the same motivation. (It can be presumed that those who

† Boston in 1980. Come on, Malzberg, bite the bullet.
‡ In *The Jewel-Hinged Jaw*, Samuel R. Delany writes that the primary motivation of science fiction editors is to be assured that they are not doing anything wrong. "Since I cannot grant them this assurance I stay away from most of them."
* Of course writers at the top are at the mercy of no one. They write what they wish. The point is that they got to the top by writing, deliberately or from cunning, that which intersected closely with what was perceived as safe and they are not now capable of writing otherwise, if they ever wanted to. Most, to their increase, never did.

feel or function differently find it almost impossible to get their work into the mass market.) They must produce that which will not offend, which will not cause an editor to question the commercial viability of a book, a process leading quickly to rejection. Science fiction, like all commercial fiction (and quality lit too although in a slightly different way), can perhaps be best understood in terms of what is *not* written rather than what is. Self-censorship controls. Any writer who understands this at all will know what not to try. As good a definition of professionalism as any other.

What *is* unsaleable then? What are the taboos and limitations which have been imposed upon the field? No list can be inclusive, of course (new circumstances lead to new taboos; Larry Janifer recalls a sex book publisher of the early sixties who, keeping close eye through lawyers on the courts, would have a new list of *do's* and *don'ts* issued every *week*; quite difficult if one had a novel-in-progress), but for general edification a partial list can be prepared. It must be made clear that the list is not immutable; it is only the fact of taboo which is constant. Buggery may come and pinko liberalism may go; old terrors will become cuddly rabbits and new beasts with rotten teeth will ease in through the windows. Even so, there will always be in this field (as in all others) certain subjects which can on only extraordinary occasions be discussed, certain approaches which can only be taken at the highest risk.

Some decades after Detroit, here is a small Common Book:

ONE: Bleak, dystopian, depressing material which implies that the present cultural fix is insane or transient and will self-destruct . . . that the very ethos and materials of the society, without the introduction of hungry invaders or Venusian outrage, will bring it down.

(The key here is *self*-destruction; there is no essential taboo against an extrapolation of the present culture which will be destroyed by the envious or by the righteous underground. The problem is an extrapolated present that without the slightest shove goes merrily to extinction. E. M. Forster's "The Machine Stops," published in 1902 in another country and anthologized endlessly in this field, strikes me as the kind of story which would be unpublishable in any contemporary science fiction magazine.)

TWO: Material which is highly internalized. That is, science fiction written from the point of view of a meditative and introspective central character whose perceptions are the central facet of the work, whose reactions to the events of the story are more important than the story itself. Goodbye Henry James, so long Herman Melville, get lost Saul Bellow; *The Demolished Man* would have a hell of a time getting sold by an unknown Alfred Bester in this market.

THREE: Science fiction which implies that contemporary accepted mores of sexuality, socioeconomics or familial patterning might be corrupting, dangerous or destructive. This appears to be a corollary to Dangerous Plot ONE but must be distinguished from it because while the first taboo would merely be against self-destructiveness, the third shuts off the possibility of serious investigation of alternatives. There has never been—as a now aged but still angry Will Sykora, chairman of the first World Science Fiction Convention in 1939, pointed out to me scant months ago—a communistic science fiction; that is, there has never been a body of work in science fiction done seriously analyzing the way a Marxian society might work (or fail to work) in the future or on any other planet. There similarly has never been a science fiction in which homosexuality or polymorphous perversity were considered as cultural norms (Charles Beaumont's 1955 "The Crooked Man" evokes a homosexual society but only in a surprise ending which is supposed to make the story horrible and, for that time and *Playboy*'s audience, probably succeeded); there has never been a science fiction in which alternatives to the nuclear family were perceived as anything other

than horrible (as they were in Gordon R. Dickson's *Dorsai!*
with its Warrior Creche, or Damon Knight's "Ask Me Anything" with its kidnapped infants' brains put into cyborgs).
In the late seventies John Varley published a few short stories
in which sex change was seen as a cultural norm, but then
again as in Wyman Guin's 1951 "Beyond Bedlam," where
schizophrenia was seen as the norm, the stories settled for a
schematization without interposing in the narrative any character who as a surrogate reader might have raised questions
on the system with which the characters—and hence the
writer—were compelled to deal.

FOUR: Science fiction which owes less to classical, Aris-
totelian notions of "plot"—the logical, progressive ordering of
events as a protagonist attempts to solve a serious and personally significant problem—than "mood" . . . that is, the events
for their own sake, perceived in chiaroscuro fashion without
the superficial ordering imposed by a central point of view or
a problem-solving format. (This would render not only
Ulysses-Finnegan's Wake influences taboo in science fiction
but would mean that even more modest experiments in form,
such as those of Donald Barthelme, Tillie Olsen or Grace
Paley, would be unacceptable . . . indeed the bewildered reaction of science fiction editors to work of this sort is to ask,
"Where's the story?" and in terms of classical perception of
plot they are, to be sure, quite right.)

FIVE: Science fiction truly at the hard edge of contemporary scientific investigation . . . science fiction which
denies Einsteinian theory, the speed of light as an absolute
limitation upon speed itself, science fiction which looks at
Darwinism in light of recent studies which indicate that the
whole question of natural selection must be reevaluated.

Editors tend to blame not themselves but the *writers* for
this, and there is a small amount of truth in this; writers, particularly commercial writers, are lazy and superficial by economic and psychic necessity. "All the science I ever needed

to know I got out of a bottle of scotch," James Blish quotes an unnamed science fiction writer in *The Issue at Hand,* and John W. Campbell in his last years complained of the reluctance or inability of new writers and old to work at the frontier of scientific investigation. Still, truly original or heretic approaches to scientific thought would unsettle the preconceived reader and editorial notions of the category. There has not been—this is an extreme generalization but I will stand by it and take objections c/o the publisher, with promise to apologize in the Second Edition if necessary—a truly original scientific extrapolation in science fiction in at least ten years. Perhaps Poul Anderson's *Tau Zero* ("To Outlive Eternity") played with notions of relativity which had been commonly accepted up until then; perhaps Bob Shaw's "Light of Other Days" offered in his slow glass an entirely new, scientifically rationalized and rigorously imagined technological imposition upon the culture. Perhaps Pamela Sargent's 1971 "The Other Perceiver," which questioned the perception of waste and the life cycle might qualify. They are the most recent examples of science fiction which can even be proposed as at the harder edge of scientific investigation, pursued with the hard edge of rigor.

SIX: Science fiction which questions science fiction; work which questions the assumptions of the category and speculates on the effect it might have upon its readership. Silverberg's two short stories and my own *Galaxies* (all cited elsewhere) are the last examples of work of this form; the most recent was published more than half a decade ago.

SEVEN: Genuinely feminist science fiction; that is, science fiction in which women are perceived to react to events and internalize in a way which is neither a culturally received stereotype (the bulk of science fiction before 1970) nor a merely male stereotype projected onto female characters. (Most of the female-protagonist work of the post-1970 period.) The women of contemporary "feminist" science fiction are not women but male characters with female names, genitalia and secondary sexual characteristics; most of the advance into the era of liberation has only been in terms of new labels for an old constituency. I have absolutely no conception of what a true feminist science fiction would be, and I am more than half-convinced that I could not write it (although ideally male writers could do it as well as female), but it would be like nothing we have seen before and would bear little relation to the gender-changed 1940s pulp envisionings which are passed off as feminist science fiction today. (The only truly feminist science fiction story I can bring to mind—which is not to say that there might not be others—is James Tiptree's [Alice Sheldon's] 1973 "The Women Men Don't See," which shows a degree of submission, subtlety and converted rage in its two female characters absolutely not glimpsed elsewhere in science fiction.)

This dismal listing—and there is no way to characterize it other than as dismal; give it to an aspirant science fiction writer and show the aspirant how to sink a career—in no way is meant to imply my own endorsement of the tabooed viewpoints. (Some are close to my gnarled little heart and others are my own anathema. Some I could write and more than a couple do not, to me, seem worth writing at all.) What I am merely suggesting is that a science fiction novel (and almost any science fiction short story other than by an important writer) flouting one or more of the taboos listed would be very unlikely to find a publisher. (It goes without saying that more than one taboo could be assaulted in a work. Bester's *The Demolished Man*, which would probably be unpublishable today, took on at least three of them; Sturgeon's long-promised novel of which the novella "When You Care/When You Love" published in 1962 is the supposed opening section might well cut through all seven.) It is what they call in Las Vegas or Atlantic City an out bet to suggest that no more than a hundred thousand words of science fiction published throughout the ensuing decade will take on any of these strictures.

And so the decade is launched. It is in fact well launched; the patterns of the eighties are well set: the conglomerates will dominate, fewer titles will receive more publicity, the magazines will drift away, the ambitious new writers will have a tough time. (When except for the brief glimmering between 1952 and 1955 did they not?) It would be easy to conclude with the clarion call for the ending of such taboos: liberation, ladies and gents, to the barricades, take on the stereotypes, muscle away the poltroons and the elitists, throw a flying fuck in the case of the Queen. Kill, kill, kill, kill, kill, kill! as Lear pointed out (hopelessly) on the heath. If not such fervid cries, at least an ironic suggestion with a moue of the features that it might have been the very taboo-laden atmosphere of the late fifties which contributed to the near collapse of the field. A similar atmosphere prevailing today might replicate the disaster unless editors become adventurous, writers daring, readers insistent and so on. Onward! Onward with liberated science fiction!

It would be nice to round it off that way but I am distinctly middle-aged and have been a professional science fiction writer for a long time. I have been reading in the field for three decades. I do not believe that I could sustain the call to barricades without collapsing into self-loathing chuckles and ironic gasps, the kind of laughter with which attendants in mental institutions and bartenders in writers' heavens all over the country are so familiar. I cannot sustain that voice because I do not believe that science fiction will ever become liberated† (what is liberation?) or that if the ragged old form did that it would be to its advantage.

To the contrary. A true science fiction might destroy the

---

† Liberation would take down the walls. No more science fiction. No more *Analog*, world sf conventions, First Fandom, portions and outlines or editorial lunches. Just a bunch of writers among a larger bunch of writers, none of them being read by anyone. For God's sake, up the walls of the world!

field commercially, sending the majority of its readership away in confusion or horror. They do not read science fiction, most of them, to be disturbed but to be pacified. Science fiction indeed may be flourishing now precisely to the degree that it is saying less and saying it worse than ever before. The period of greatest economic and readership growth in the history of the field has coincided with the post-1975 shutdown of experimentation or ideological quibble. Science fiction has become big business; it intersects with the media which are feeding it and which it has fed so well, and the field is being run with negligible exceptions amongst the minor book publishers and the magazines by the very same people. Gulf & Western and Rocket Industries. The Music Corporation of Speculation. International Telephone & Terrestials.

And brave, brave new decade to the inheritors of the mantle of Kornbluth and Kuttner and Campbell. Could the twenty-seven-year-old John W. Campbell get a job today anywhere in the industry? Would they let Horace stay in his apartment while the galleys were slipped underneath the door?

1979/1980: New Jersey

The Richard Nixon-John B. Mitchell-
Spiro Agnew Blues

Science fiction is not necessarily a cultural microcosm (and
then again perhaps it is; the boys in the back room of the
fifties indeed felt they were building a better world), but
confluence in the political life of the Republic and the
market news was striking in the mid-seventies. The collapse
of the market for "experimental," "literary," "avant-garde,"
"downbeat," "technophobic" or "depressing" science fiction
can be placed within virtually a month of Nixon's speedy and
insufficiently dramatic eviction from high office; by the end
of 1974 the editorial doors had closed. Writers and work em-
bodying the cutting edge of the field through the seventies
were not having their calls returned, editors who had become
identified with those writers and work were either losing their
jobs or frantically changing policy. Gerald Ford and the era
of Lucas seemed to descend upon the Republic simultaneously; we know that this was not true (Ford was gone
when *Star Wars* opened in the spring of 1977), but it *feels*
true. Post-Watergate was when Lucas was raising the money,
anyway.

This, to be sure, is a perilous statement . . . retrospection
seeks order that the ongoing reality had no time to set . . .
but this matter of perceiving science fiction as a microcosm
of the nation's tumultuous, self-deluded and ultimately disastrous politics must be briefly pursued. I have felt for a while
that the eviction of Nixon was the last gasp of the contemporary left; after fifteen years of assassinations, demon-

strations, murmurings, rumbles and license, a President had actually been thrown out of office legally and the left wing recoiled as if in horror: they had, like the child in tantrum who burns down the place, never really expected that they could get away with it. Simultaneously, the right wing and great center regarded the detenancy as the last concession that the left wing would exact. "We gave you the son of a bitch," seemed to be the implicit statement, "you made such an all-fired nuisance of yourselves that we let him go but I'm telling you for your own good: this is the last time. You kids have pulled your last prank; now it's time to go out and get a job."

All the kids seemed to get the message. By 1976 Eugene McCarthy was a ghost candidate, the left wing of the Democratic party (as "represented" by the pusillanimous and disgraced Humphrey) could not even go through the motions of a primary fight, and the "liberal" Republicans had assented to the removal of Nelson Rockefeller from the vice presidency without protest. The antiwar movement had long since fragmented and collapsed and the war itself if not over was over for us. The sixties radicals were dead, in hiding, on the underside or taking up permanent rights via squatting in the middle class.

And in science fiction, *simil.*

In science fiction, the speed and force of the counterrevolution was so abrupt that many of the younger writers for years thereafter were still writing short stories and novels for a market which no longer existed. The bottom of the original anthology market fell out. Ballantine Science Fiction became Del Rey Books and proceeded in both theory and reissued fact to reconstruct the childhood of Lester del Rey. Random House quit science fiction and Pyramid quit everything and those publishers which continued were letting the word out explicitly that traditional themes and handling would be appreciated. Aldiss and Ballard fell out of the American market; Ellison, Silverberg and the undersigned announced within a fortnight of one another in late 1975* that we would write science fiction no more, and new writers began to have more trouble finding publishers than at any time since the early sixties. Certain kinds of writing were almost unsaleable.

It is easy—almost seductively easy one might say—by pursuing this line of confluence to say that science fiction was merely reacting to or reenacting on its own level the political climate of its time. I am not quite sure that this is so; science fiction has been a fairly self-contained circumstance since its inception whose development often moved at odds with the larger culture. (The first half of the forties, that decade of unspeakable horror, will always be known in science fiction as the "Golden Age.") Rather, serendipity seems to be the issue; for different reasons both America and science fiction found itself in retreat from the shocks and terrors of the sixties, which as they brought the very existence of institutions into question, opened the windows on a future which was unacceptable.

The assassinations, the war, the corruption of all political life, the decline of religion, the rise of divorce and sexual libertarianism had opened up the same trap doors that the post-technological visions of Ballard and Aldiss, the psychological horrors of Tiptree and the demented idealism of Lafferty had opened in science fiction, and both America (its corporate structure and institutions) and science fiction (through editors and publishers) were in fear of falling. In both cases, the forces of counterrevolution had the same desperate, unspoken assent; no one really wanted to see the country or this great escape fiction fall apart. That the President of the United States could be revealed as a simple crook, that the literature of technological transcendence should become imbued with images of how the machines were killing

---

* We've all reneged—Silverberg published a long novel, *Lord Valentine's Castle* in early 1980 and is at work on others; Ellison has published several stories in the genre and contracted out a few novels; I've done enough short stories to make up another book . . . but editors and publishers know what lying swine writers are, anyway, so no harm done.

us was simply too much for the audience to handle. Blame them not. Their confusion became hostility and finally outrage: Nixon might be thrown out and the visions of Ballard scribbled like graffiti all over the holy gates, but now things were going to get back to normal, as quickly as possible. And they were going to stay normal for a hell of a long time. There were big plans to put everything on hold once the temple was resecured.

It may turn around again. It may not. Years ago, the theory of cycles would apply in politics and science fiction alike and one could make reference to the metaphor of the pendulum. A society and economy controlled by conglomerates, however, a literature which is a minor subdivision of a subdivision of these conglomerates can be manipulated to stay frozen in position (until or unless the whole thing falls apart), and in this totalitarian possibility science fiction and American life can be seen at last to become indistinguishable, to become facets of one another in the last fifth of the last century of the last millennium in which the theory of causality can be seen (or may be needed) at all to apply.

1980: New Jersey

Cornell George Hopley Woolrich:
December 1903 to September 1968

At the end, in the last year, he looked three decades older. The booze had wrecked him, the markets had wrecked him, *he* had wrecked him; by the time that friends dragged him out in April to St. Clare's Hospital where they took off the gangrenous leg, he had the stunned aspect of the very old. Where there had been edges there was now only the gelatinous material that when probed would not rebound.

Nonetheless, if the booze had stripped all but bone it had left his eyes moist and open, childlike and vulnerable. That September in the open coffin, surrounded by flowers sent by the Chase Manhattan Bank, he looked young; he looked like the man who in his late twenties had loafed around the ballrooms and written of the debutantes.

There were five names in the guest book, Leo and Cylvia Margulies of *Mike Shayne's Mystery Magazine* leading off. Leo died in December 1975 and Cylvia divested herself of the publication about two years later.

He died in print. The April 1968 *Escapade* had a story, and *Ellery Queen's Mystery Magazine* had taken his stunning "New York Blues" to publish it two years later; that novelette had been written in late 1967. Ace Books had embarked upon an ambitious program of reissue which brought *The Bride Wore Black, Rendezvous in Black, Phantom Lady,* and others back into the mass market. Truffaut's *The Bride Wore Black* was in production. The Ellery Queen hardcover mystery annual had a story. Now, more than a decade later, he is out of print; an item for the specialty and university presses, an occasional republication in an Ellery Queen annual. Ace let the books go a long time past: poor sales. There are no other paperbacks. The hardcovers—what few copies remain—are for the collectors.

"It isn't dying I'm afraid of, it isn't that at all; I know what it is to die, I've died already. It is the endless obliteration, the knowledge that there will never be anything else. That's what I can't stand, to try so hard and to end in nothing. You know what I mean, don't you? . . . I really loved to write."

His mother Claire died in 1956. Shortly thereafter his own work virtually ceased. A novel—never published—found with his effects; it had been rejected all over New York in the early sixties. A few short stories for *Ellery Queen* and *The Saint Mystery Magazine*. His relationship with his mother had been the central—it is theorized that it was the only—relationship of his life; they had lived together continuously for her last fourteen years. When she died he lived alone in one room on the second floor of the Sheraton-Russell Hotel in Manhattan surrounded by cases and cases of beer cans and bottles of whiskey, and invited the staff to come up and drink with him and watch television. Sometimes he would sit in the lobby; more occasionally he would take a cab to McSorley's Tavern in the village. The gangrene which came from an ill-fitting shoe and which untreated turned his left leg to charcoal, slowly, from early 1967 to April 1968, ended all that; he would stay in his room and drink almost all the time and stare at the television looking for a film from one of his novels or short stories which came on often enough and usually after 2 A.M.; between the movies and the alcohol he was finally able to find sleep. For a few hours. Until ten or eleven in the morning, when it would all start again. At the end he had almost none of his books left in the room: he had given them all away to casual visitors. Bellboys. Maids. The night manager. An employee of his literary agent. He could not bear to have his work around him any more.

"I got six hundred dollars from Alfred Hitchcock for the movie rights to 'Rear Window.' That's all that I got; it was one story in a collection of eight that was sold in the forties by the agent H. N. Swanson for five thousand dollars; he sold *everything* for five thousand dollars; that's why we all called him five grand Swannie. But that didn't bother me really; what bothered me was that Hitchcock wouldn't even send me a ticket to the premiere in New York. He knew where I lived. He wouldn't even send me a ticket."

The novels were curiously cold for all of their effects and mercilessly driven, but the characters, particularly the female characters, who were the protagonists of many of them, were rendered with great sensitivity and were always in enormous pain. That was one of the mysteries of Woolrich's work for the editors and writers who knew him: how could a man who could not relate to women at all, who had had a brief and terrible marriage annulled when he was twenty-five, who had lived only alone or with his mother since . . . how could such a man have had such insight into women, write of them with such compassion, make these creatures of death and love dance and crumple on the page? Some theorized that the writer could identify with these women because that was the terrible and essential part of him which could never be otherwise acknowledged. Others simply called it a miracle: a miracle that a lonely man in a hotel room could somehow create, populate and justify the world.

"I tried to move out. In 1942 I lived alone in a hotel room for three weeks and then one night she called me and said, 'I can't live without you, I must live with you, I need you,' and I put down the phone and I packed and I went back to that place and for the rest of her life I never spent a night away from her, not one. I know what they thought of me, what they said about me but I just didn't care. I don't regret it and I'll never regret it as long as I live."

He began as a minor imitator of Fitzgerald, wrote a novel in the late twenties which won a prize, became dissatisfied with his work and stopped writing for a period of years. When he came back it was to *Black Mask* and the other detective magazines with a curious and terrible fiction which had never been seen before in the genre markets; Hart Crane and certainly Hemingway were writing of people on the edge of their emotions and their possibilities, but the genre mystery markets were filled with characters whose pain was circumstantial, whose resolution was through action; Woolrich's gallery was of those so damaged that their lives could only be seen as vast anticlimaxes to central and terrible events which had occurred long before the incidents of the story. Hammett and his great disciple Chandler had verged toward this more than a little; there is no minimizing the depth of their contribution to the mystery and to literature, but Hammett and Chandler were still working within the devices of their category: detectives confronted problems and solved (or more commonly failed to solve) them, evil was generalized but had at least specific manifestations. Woolrich went far out on the edge. His characters killed, were killed, witnessed murder, attempted to solve it, but the events were peripheral to the central circumstances. What I am trying to say, perhaps, is that Hammett and Chandler wrote *of* death, but the novels and short stories of Woolrich *were* death—in all of its delicacy and grace, its fragile beauty as well as its finality.

Most of his plots made no objective sense. Woolrich was writing at the cutting edge of his time. Twenty years later his vision would attract Truffaut, whose own influences had been the philosophy of Sartre and the French *nouvelle vague*, the central conception that nothing really mattered. Nothing at all . . . but the suffering. Ah, that mattered; that mattered quite a bit.

"I wasn't that good you know. What I was was a guy who could write a little publishing in magazines surrounded by people who couldn't write at all. So I looked pretty good. But I never thought I was that good at all. All that I thought was that I tried."

Inevitably, his vision verged toward the fantastic; he published a scattering of stories which appeared to conform to that genre at least to the degree that the fuller part of his vision could be seen as "mysteries." For Woolrich it *all* was fantastic; the clock in the tower, hand in the glove, out of control vehicle, errant gunshot which destroyed; whether destructive coincidence was masked in the "naturalistic" or the "incredible" was all pretty much the same to him. *Rendezvous in Black, The Bride Wore Black, Nightmare* are all great swollen dreams, turgid constructions of the night, obsession and grotesque outcome; to turn from these to the "fantastic" was not to turn at all. The work, as is usually the case with a major writer, was perfectly formed, perfectly consistent; the vision leached into every area and pulled the book together. "Jane Brown's Body" is a suspense story. *The Bride Wore Black* is science fiction. *Phantom Lady* is a gothic. *Rendezvous in Black* was a *bildungsroman*. It does not matter.

"I'm glad you liked *Phantom Lady* but I can't help you, you see. I can't accept your praise. The man who wrote that novel died a long, long time ago. He died a long, long time ago."

At the end, amidst the cases and the bottles and the empty glasses as the great black leg became turgid and began to stink, there was nothing at all. The television did not help, the whiskey left no stain, the bellhops could not bring distraction. They carried him out to St. Clare's and cut off the leg in April and sent him back in June with a prosthesis; the doctors were cheerful. "He has a chance," they said. "It all depends upon his will to live." At the Sheraton-Russell they came to his doors with trays, food, bottles, advice. They took good care of him. They helped him on his crutches to the lobby and put him in the plush chair at the near door so that he could see lobby traffic. They were unfailingly kind. They brought him into the dining room and brought him out. They took him upstairs. They took him downstairs. They stayed with him. They created a network of concern: the Woolrich network in the Sheraton-Russell.

In September, like Delmore Schwartz, he had a stroke in a hotel corridor; in September, like Schwartz in an earlier August, he died instantly. He lay in the Campbell funeral parlor in a business suit for three days surrounded by flowers from Chase Manhattan.

His will left $850,000 to Columbia University (he had inherited money; the markets didn't leave him much) to establish a graduate creative writing program in memory of Claire. He had been a writer of popular fiction, had never had a serious review in the United States, had struggled from cheap pulp magazines to genre hardcover and paperback. Sure he wanted respectability; a university cachet. Sure. Why not? Who wouldn't?

"Life is death. Death is in life. To hold your own true love in your arms and see the skeleton she will be; to know that your love leads to death, that death is all there is, that is what I know and what I do not want to know and what I cannot bear. Don't leave me. Don't leave me.

"Don't leave me now, Barry."

1980: New Jersey

A Few Hard Truths for the Troops

ONE: There is no substitute for personal editorial contact in this business, particularly at the outset of a career. It is easy enough to sell short stories by mail, but in order to sell them in any quantity the editors should be met; it is ten times easier to sell a first novel to an editor who knows you. Shortly after the initial sales, therefore, it is imperative for a new writer to come to New York (wherein work almost all the editors), or, better yet, to attend the science fiction conventions. The editors go to them. There are at least five conventions a year—the world convention, the west coast convention on the July 4 weekend, the New York convention in the spring, the Philadelphia and Cincinnati conventions—at which half the editors or more are present. Although a new writer should not become obsessed with convention attendance, at least six should be attended in the year after the first sale (assuming any professional ambitions and spare funds at all), and at least three a year thereafter.

It *is* possible to run a career from a post office box—James Tiptree, Jr. (Alice Sheldon) is the most notable recent example as Cordwainer Smith (Paul Linebarger) was of the past—but only a couple of such careers exist during any given writing generation (which according to van Vogt, and I agree, is just about ten years). The rest of you—the rest of *us*—are like it or not going to have to make the changes, work the scenery. Ten years ago or more a young writer would be best advised to come to New York to live for a while, but New York is now such an expensive and (for many) fundamentally untenable place that it is no longer necessary. With writers scattered throughout the countryside editors have a good excuse to spend expense account money to go to conventions to see them and editors have no objection to this.

TWO: Reviews have almost no effect upon the sale of a science fiction book. Prepublication reviews in the trade journals are meaningless; reviews in the professional and amateur magazines appear so long after publication that the fate of a book has long been decided by the time they appear. The only factor affecting the sale of a science fiction novel from the point of view of the publisher is print order; a book that prints more will sell more, assuming a certain rough fixed percentage of copies printed as sales, and therefore the destiny of a book has been resolved before it is even out of manuscript. Print order is in itself determined by the amount of the advance—the more a publisher has paid the more he must print in order to retrieve the advance—and the advance depends upon the reputation of the writer, editorial caprice, the editorial-book interface, the general state of the market and so on. (Merit except for a rare case or two has *no* effect upon the advance.) There have been cases in which books for which large advances have been paid have had small print orders and failed dismally; this is because either the editor has, in the interim, lost his job or because others in the hierarchy are out to sink him. There are even fewer cases in which books with small advances have had large print orders, but here venery and caprice are the *only* applicable factors and it is impossible to do anything about them.

THREE: Although matters have changed somewhat in the last half decade, science fiction is still regarded by the nonspecialist publishers as a minor category and the science fiction editor is low in relative standing; this means for all intents and purposes that if a writer's editor is fired or quits his job the writer is finished with the publisher . . . the writer simply has no individual cachet for the publisher; he is an anonymous part of someone's "science fiction list." Accordingly one does not cultivate publishers but *editors*, and if one is fortunate one's editor will remain at a post for a long time acquiring autonomy and prestige, *or* will go onto other publishers at an increasing level of responsibility, finally achieving a position of full autonomy.

FOUR: There is no point in trying to construct a saleable novel by studying and then reproducing material which (even if recently published) is already on the stands or in the bookstores; the reality of publishing, because of the nature of the production and editorial processes, is at least two years ahead of books being published today (and the books two years behind). Attempts to reproduce the mood, subject or style of freshly successful writers is only to remind the editors of what naïfs they were a couple of years ago, and besides, they already *have* published stuff like that. You are far better off trying to reproduce the sense, subject and style of much older work, the forties and fifties novels; that is where the field reposes and probably always will. (You are almost certainly doomed if you attempt at the beginning of your career to do truly innovative, original work. You will not sell it. You may scatter a few such short stories here and there but the novel market is blocked to you. The time to do innovative work if you are fool enough to want to is after you have sold a few novels, have some kind of cachet in the field and have enabled the publishers to presume that you have an audience which is looking for your work and which you can take along with you. The publishers are wrong in this judgement, but they are wrong in most of their judgements, and simple, vulnerable, hapless creatures are not necessarily to be condemned for that.)

FIVE: Never try to sell a novel to a publisher on the basis that although another publisher has rejected it it has done so with a "good," i.e., glowing, letter of rejection extolling the merits of the proposal and regretting only its inappropriateness for the particular list. Publishers tend to believe one another (otherwise why would they hire the same editors, publish the same writers, work from the same pool of free-lance artists and copy editors), and a letter of rejection in any guise is nothing more than that. The only way to sell a novel in early (and usually in late) career is to represent it as new work, never offered to the marketplace before.

SIX: On balance, and taking everything into account, including the residual rights, the small notoriety, the sexual prerogatives occasionally available at conventions, the shelf of collected works and the feeling of accomplishment, not disregarding all of this but putting it in the balance, you would be better off going to law school . . . or if that is not your thing, becoming a temporary typist.

1980: New Jersey

Onward and Upward With the Arts
Part III

When I started off in this field in 1967, just a plucky lad with a sack over my shoulder, off to Ferman and Wollheim to seek my fortune, it all seemed very reasonable. The fact that no one had ever done it did not occur to me at the time or for several years thereafter: what I would do would be to write science fiction of such imposing quality and quantity that sooner or later it would seep into *The New York Review of Books*, *The New York Times Book Review* and *The Hudson Review*, not the *fiction* you understand (later for the *Hudson*, but the recognition. "My," I conceived of Phillip Rahv saying, breathing hard, brandishing Lancer Book X3418-B ISBN 0075, "this isn't your ordinary science fiction full of monsters and stuff, this is quality *lit*. Let's give this boy the *push*." Soon thereafter there would be "At Home with Malzberg" sidebars accompanying the review of the new novel (surely from Farrar, Straus now), "Oh, I don't know," I would say with a fetching little laugh, tossing my head and inserting yet another cigarette into my elegant black holder, "I don't know if I'm all that good; you have to understand that I'm just one of many. Many, many fine writers.

"Why this field is *filled* with people who are doing literature, you might never be able to guess it from the magazine and paperback covers in which they're forced to appear because of the economics of the paperback original market . . . but they're quite as good as anybody writing in America today. Why, just for openers there's A and B and then there's C, terrific kindly old fellow who has quietly been doing wonderful work for the penny-a-word market for decades, and let's not forget D, who has been underrated for so long and whose new serial in *Worlds of If* is really terrific, and then as long as I'm making a list you ought to investigate E and F and G———"

I had resolved to be generous, you understand. I knew of all the sullen, recriminative successes embittered by years of struggle and anonymity who held onto their recognition like spoiled children and would not share even a bite of it. I had been impressed by the stories of Robert Frost and Ezra Pound, determined to be unlike the former, who would not say a good word for any living poet, just like the latter, who told his Parisian publisher that if the choice was between doing *The Wasteland* or his own new volume, the Eliot work should be done. What must be understood about that twenty-eight-year-old version of myself is that although I was a fool, I was a fool of the kindliest nature. I really did not want to persevere or succeed at the cost of others, and if I did it was my intention to pass around at least a little bit of the success. (My first Ace paperback of short stories paid tribute in its introduction to several science fiction writers who I felt were superior to me.)

I *was* a fool of course. An idiot stick has been described as pointing toward nowhere on one end, attached to an idiot on the other, and the stick was science fiction. In 1967 no science fiction writer who stayed within the confines of the genre had ever received critical recognition or significant commercial success. Kurt Vonnegut, Jr. had published with some frequency in the field in the fifties of course (and knew as much about it as, say, Robert Sheckley), but he had begun in the middle of the decade to disassociate himself from science fiction as vocally and persistently as he could; his denials that he was a science fiction writer and his refusal to publish his books under category imprint or his stories in the genre magazines had, along with good acquaintanceship, put him in the position finally in 1968 with the publication of *Slaughterhouse Five* to find recognition and enormous audience as a "serious" writer. Richard McKenna's first publications were all science fiction short stories (and several of them were outstanding), but his first novel, *The Sand Pebbles*, was of course a near-date historical and was serialized in *The Saturday Evening Post* and picked up by the book clubs without even the knowledge that he had published in the field. Ray Bradbury had at least started off within the genre but soon enough his stories, all rejected (but one) by John W. Campbell, were appearing in the bottom-line pulp magazines and *Weird Tales*, and then in one postwar burst in the mass-circulation magazines; *The Martian Chronicles* was regarded as the work of a fantasist who had had only glancing acquaintance with science fiction, and Bradbury's ascent came via the best-of-the-year short story collections, script work and *Playboy* magazine. No other writer who had published in quantity in the genre had, as of 1967, had even a whiff of serious attention from the academic critics or the quarterlies.

The question arises soon enough—it always has when I have discussed this issue in public or even in small, clamorous trysts in restaurants or bars—as to exactly why I wanted critical recognition and what that critical recognition, then or now, would have been worth in terms of audience, income or general kharmic peace. The answer is one I would prefer to table within this context; the question is not contemptible and the answer may have to do more with my own personal conflicts and difficulties than it does with market realities. For the moment it is sufficient to say that no serious writer can be taken seriously in his time (and usually for all time) unless the academic critics pay him some attention, and I felt then (I am not nearly so sure now) that I was a serious writer. With the general trade imprints, the O. Henry Awards collection or the college anthologies closed to my science fiction, there was no chance of achieving reputation for the work that I had elected to do . . . I could have, in somewhat Vonnegut-fashion, ceased to write science fiction and come at the academies from a different direction, but I did not think that was quite fair . . . I would have had to partly repudiate and totally abandon the work that I cared to do and was doing well. So simple equity and justice were one motivation, and the other was that if I had achieved critical attention I might have had at least the option of finding a university teaching position, a cachet absolutely unavailable to a science fiction writer at that time. (Matters have changed since then but not too greatly.)

Whether my ambitions were totally self-deluded or otherwise, it has been interesting (if that is the word) to survive this subsequent decade and a half as an identifiably science fiction writer and observe what has happened, to see if anyone (I obviously did not and probably never will) did break through. Over these years more than a few science fiction writers—Heinlein, Silverberg, Haldeman, Benford, Pournelle, Niven, to name less than half—have obtained huge (by late-sixties standards) advances and large or at least larger audiences, but although science fiction has clearly proven itself to be at least an intermittently commercially viable medium for a mass-market book, the question of critical recognition seems to be in the same place, relative to the field, that it was long before "Star Trek," *Star Wars, Alien* or *The Empire Strikes Back.* Only two science fiction writers in the last decade did attract widespread attention from critics and editors not already close to the form and neither of them obtained that from work done within the genre. Ursula K. Le Guin won the 1972 National Book Award in children's literature for a fantasy series; Stanislaw Lem, a Pole, attracted the attention of Theodore Solataroff for a series of novels reissued by Avon, the most recent of which was (at the time the 1977 front page *New York Times Book Review* article appeared) almost a decade old. Le Guin, a winner of the National Book Award, and Lem, an Eastern European fantasist struggling to do a body of work between the interstices of official repression, were hardly examples of the crowd bellying around in *Analog* or Doubleday Science Fiction or even the small science fiction lists of Random House or Harper & Row at the time.*

The truism seems to hold right through the eighties: no science fiction writer will ever be recognized as a writer of literary stature *for work done within the confines of the genre.*† There are reasons for this; Gregory Benford has summarized them quite neatly: the critics have nothing to gain and everything to lose by saying that they like science fiction. Taking a postion in favor of the unfamiliar would involve risk. Also—and less abstractedly—the majority of advertising revenue for the book reviews, book pages and the quarterlies comes from publishers and titles which are not science fiction. There is none of the implied economic lever which the category's editors or publishers could bring against the review media such as what a literarily oriented publisher such as Farrar, Straus or Knopf could bring against the *Times* or *The New York Review of Books*.

For a good many reasons it is probably always going to be this way. A lot of talent—not all of it; many science fiction writers do not have my mind set but some do—is going to get broken in the process, but why the hell should the critics or their media give a damn about talent? The publishers do not; the editors, most of them, can hardly under a clear light understand the difference . . . and writers who are not self-deluded fools learn in the medium long run not to care.

1980: New Jersey

---

* Harper & Row is Ursula Le Guin's publisher.
† Thomas M. Disch at this writing (September 1980) seems to have a small chance of being the significant exception . . . Disch has published much work in the prestige quarterlies (*Paris Review*, etc.), however, and it is this that has granted cachet to the science fiction, not the other way around.

Science Fiction As Picasso

Consider: perhaps not five hundred careers or a thousand but one; not all the myriad voices but one voice, not the individual struggles and destinies but the single arc of a single creator now in the middle of its sixth decade. All of the voices mingling, murmuring into one, overtones in a great chord. Science fiction as one artist. Science fiction—if you will—as Picasso.

It is not the artifacts but the vision, not the material but the theme which dominates. This has been pointed out before: it is not an original insight. Science fiction, Fred Pohl has said, is the only genre in which collaboration is commonplace, in which collaborative works of quality are prevalent because science fiction is a pool of ideas, a manner of approach; writers function less from their idiosyncratic vision (as is the case in "serious" literature) or their ability to recombine elements of the form (the mystery and western) than from their immersion in the approach. Science fiction, as Pohl said, as was recollected much earlier here, *is a way of thinking about things*. And that way was the subtext of the form from the beginning. We or they were going to get ourselves. But good. But awfully good.

Science fiction as a single, demented, multitentacled artist singing and painting and transcribing in fashion clumsy and elegant, errant and imitative, innovative and repetitious, the way the future would feel. Science fiction, born in 1926, dreaming through its childhood in the 1930s, achieving change of voice and the beginning of adult features in 1939, shooting through adolescence in the forties with all of the misdirected energy and hints of promise, arriving at a shaky legal maturity at the end of that decade with the expansion of the market and the full incorporation of a range of style and technique. Young adult in the sixties with the knowledge turned loose in a hundred ways, some toward no consequence, others foreshadowing maturity. Science fiction at thirty-five, eligible to be President! Productive of fluency. Science fiction at forty in the mid-sixties with all the hints of mid-life panic . . . chaos, fragmentation, the replication of childhood, the donning of new masks.

Science fiction, settling from its decade of panic in the mid-seventies to pursue what it had passed over when young, reworking the familiar in thoroughgoing fashion. Science fiction now at the threshold of old age, the faint whiff of alcohol and decadence as it trudges toward the millennium. Science fiction, that demented artist of which we are all but cells and cilia. Blood and bone.

Picasso went on and on, from blue period to rose, from the cubist to the surreal to the classical to the querulous serenity of old age, interrupted by flashes of self-loathing and mockery. He was not the greatest of artists but had the greatest of careers; he might have been the only painter of the first rank who was able to articulate his vision to its fullest range and implication through all of the chronology that he could have expected, able to move his career in embrace with his life until the two of them, not disjointed, could end together. Science fiction will live longer than Picasso—barring the apocalypse our little category is going to survive 2019—and it remains to be seen how the Ticketron holders and curators of the third millennia, as they poke around our own museum, will take our works, but this much is clear.

This much is clear: we may be less than the sum of our parts but we are far, far more in the aggregate than individually we ever took ourselves to be. None of us can build science fiction, none of us can destroy it. Science fiction gave us voice and the voice, however directed, must be toward its perpetuation. The Picasso of the late nineteen-sixties savagely drawing blood from *Les Demoiselles D'Avignon* caused only his own veins to sing while the painting, cool and beyond caring, hung on the walls of the Museum of Modern Art for all the crowd to see, to pity the twisted but beckoning harlots.

1980: New Jersey

Mark Clifton:
1906–1963

Kuttner died of a heart attack in his sleep, Kornbluth died of either a massive cerebral hemorrhage or a heart attack (depending upon whose version you accept), Clifton had had a bad heart for a long time. It drove him out of industry and undid him at a relatively young age. But I think that the death certificates of all three should have listed *science fiction* under cause of death. H. Beam Piper, our only suicide, blew out his brains with a shotgun in the fall of 1964 but it did not appear to be the field itself that had done it to him: the sudden death of his agent, monies tied up, depression, a big gun collection. Kuttner, Kornbluth and Clifton took it straight.

Cause of death: *science fiction*. You bet, Mark.

Kuttner and Kornbluth remain fairly prominent more than two decades after their passage (Kornbluth largely through the collaborations with Frederik Pohl and Pohl's devoted effort to keep his collaborations and collaborator in print; Kuttner because enough contemporary writers and editors remember his ten best stories enough to constantly anthologize them), but Clifton is a lost figure and it is he who needs an *amicus curiae*, court of last resort or not. His 1956 novelette "Clerical Error" was reprinted in *Neglected Visions* (and I should say they were and are; the book did not do well but the title was self-fulfilling prophecy), a Doubleday anthology coedited with Martin H. Greenberg, and under Greenberg's aegis and my own his first collection of short stories in his own language has recently been published by Southern Illinois University Press, but these frail attempts at restoration are absolutely on the margin. Clifton is unknown not only to the contemporary science fiction audience but to its writers and editors; most editors under thirty have never heard of him, most writers under forty have never read him. This is unpleasant—who of us could find this a reasonable outcome? Even *Amazing*'s mid-fifties stable of space-typists had their pride and reasonable ambitions and some fulfilled them—but it becomes genuinely wrenching when it is stated flatly (and the old-timers will verify) that for a period of four years Mark Clifton was perhaps the most prominent and controversial science fiction writer through the entire range of the magazines . . . and the early fifties for science fiction was a magazine market.

Clifton retired in 1951 after two decades as a practicing industrial psychologist (he did employment interviews and did interviews of recalcitrant workers as part of management's attempt, apparently, to control unionism), partly because of precarious health after an early heart attack and partly out of a genuine desire to not only be a writer but a science fiction writer. Between May 1952 and his death Clifton published three novels and about twenty-five short stories in the science fiction magazines, nearly a third of them written in collaboration with Frank Rylovich and Alex Apostolides. (There is some question as to how much input the collaborators really had; Rylovich published a few stories in *Worlds of If*, one of which was in a best-of-the-year collection, but Apostolides, at least under that name, published nothing elsewhere before or since.) The first of the novels, *They'd Rather Be Right* (published later by Gnome Press as *The Forever Machine*) in collaboration with Rylovich won the second science fiction novel Hugo awarded in 1955 at the Cleveland World Convention; the other two, *When They Came from Space* (1962) and *Eight Keys to Eden* (1960), were hardly as successful.

Most of the short stories upon which his reputation was

based were published in the first four years of Clifton's career. Over his last six years only a few stories saw print (none in *Astounding*, his major market), along with the unsuccessful later novels. Well before his death, in other words, Clifton had ceased to be a major figure. Diminished output was certainly the reason but whether the output was truly diminished or whether Clifton was merely being heavily rejected is speculative. It is possible (I have no direct evidence but private correspondence to another writer which I have seen may indicate) that like Cyril M. Kornbluth, Clifton's increasing ambition and sophistication caused him to write himself clear out of the magazine markets of his time . . . which were in the later fifties in a period of attrition and eventually collapsed anyway.

Long divorced and with a daughter who is (to this day) unlocatable, Mark Clifton died intestate. This made it impossible for publishers or anthology editors to negotiate for his work for years, and by the time that the newly formed SFWA and Forrest J. Ackerman had gotten some hold on the situation by the late sixties many years had passed and Clifton's time was lost. "What Have I Done?" in the Harrison-Aldiss *Astounding/Analog Reader* and "Clerical Error" in *Neglected Visions* are two of the very few reprintings of his work in the seventies and although the Donning Company, a small publisher, has announced its intention to republish *The Forever Machine*, that novel has, at this writing, been out of print in this country for at least two decades.

This litany, a *Yizkor* chant, which with minor revisions could be said over the graves of most of us (and in due course, I can assure, will be said over all of us), is what the writing of popular fiction is all about, to be sure. It would be easy to reel off the names of twenty science fiction writers almost as prominent as Clifton in his decade who are similarly unknown today. But what makes Clifton's topple from the center so painful is that within the context of the field in his time he had far to fall and it must have been extremely painful for him because it all happened during his lifetime. By the end of the fifties, barely able to write, hardly able to sell, he had already lost the entire sense of his career.

And he was good.

He was, in fact, in a particular way the best of them all. Clifton knew what technology was going to do to people; he spotted the fifties as the decade when those effects would become institutionalized, and he wrote about angst, the alienation effect and the seepage of the human spirit through the machines with detachment, precision and a good deal of control. Never better than an adequate stylist, he painfully improved his technique through the years and by the mid-fifties was writing quite well, far above the range of most contributors to *Astounding*. It was at that point that he began to get into sales trouble.

What the private correspondence indicates is that Clifton, a pained and sophisticated man who came into science fiction as an artistic naïf seeing it as the medium which would change the world, and who went out of it a decade later bitterly convinced that the nature of its editors and its audience forever delimited the field and made it beneath contempt as a serious means of social or political thought . . . what this correspondence indicates is that Clifton, whose career paralleled the decade in its collapse from optimism to despair, understood everything that had happened to him and would not have been surprised at all by his subsequent obscurity. What comes off in those letters is a powerful sense of disgust and self-loathing—Clifton hated himself for ever having invested science fiction with expectation. In the early fifties he saw it as mutant literature for mutant, special types who bound together would order the cosmos, and by the mid-fifties he was railing about the parasitic behavior of the West Coast fans who attached themselves to a notably immature and unsophisticated literary agent, all of them calling for the return of science fiction to the creed of adventure.

The letters are extraordinarily interesting in their portrait of a first-rate mind of mature wisdom proceeding very rapidly from self-delusion to existential despair. It is a sad thing—but in honoring the dead also, perhaps, an act of great compassion—that they must never be published.

Like virtually every science fiction writer of his time—John Clute has pointed this out in a sensitive essay on Cyril M. Kornbluth—Clifton showed a curious inability to do his best work at novel length. This may have had to do with the exigencies of the magazine market, or with the fact that virtually all of the science fiction of the fifties was conceived and written for magazine publication and subsequently pushed and pulled, manipulated into novel length; it may have had to do with the fact that science fiction at that time was a medium most easily adaptable to the short story, the single extrapolation worked to a single point. Whatever the reasons— and they are worth another essay—they applied in Clifton's case. His last novel, *The Forever Machine*, an outright padding of a novella, was based upon short story characters and situations which had run the previous year in *Astounding*. Even by the less than rigorous standards of those times this work must be recognized as seriously attenuated. (The plot, that of a computer-generated immortality that can only be granted if the subject gave up his preconceptions and prejudices, his very individuality, and the resistance of the masses to this Beneficent Scientific Solution, can be considered to be quintessentially fifties in theme and development; Sloan Wilson's audience for *The Man in the Grey Flannel Suit* would have been entirely comfortable with the theme if not with the machinery.) The short stories, on the other hand, were thoughtful and controlled; the later ones are quite poised and bitter, and at least "Clerical Error," "What Have I Done?" and "What Now, Little Man?" must be regarded as central to the literature. They were endlessly influential and imitated; they live on even as does "Vintage Season" or "All You Zombies" as the basis of prominent work by less original writers.

Despite the understated and occasionally clumsy style, Clifton was as innovative as Cyril Kornbluth or Alfred Bester in what he did for the field: he used the common themes—

alien invasion, encroaching technology, revolution against impenetrable bureaucracy—but he brought to them the full range of psychological insight available to a trained and sophisticated mind. His view of how individuals would deal with the institutions and devices of the technological night was never optimistic (his very first story, "What Have I Done?", depicts humanity as inalterably vile) but became steadily blacker as the decade and his own career progressed, and "Hang Head, Vandal!", his last published story, is a vision of appalling bleakness. The vandals who wrecked Mars were all of us and Clifton, putting his last two novels on the market shortly thereafter, proceeded, it would seem, not to write. He died less than two years later. The correspondence to which I have referred ceased . . . his correspondent stopped answering his letters.

There is more to be said of Clifton and someday someone will say it (those letters might be published), but here is the last to be said of him here: Mark Clifton, a major writer of his time, protégé of Campbell, Hugo winner, master of psionics, envy of the fans and colleagues for his shotgun career . . . Mark Clifton, that innovator and man of wisdom, earned for all of his science fiction in his lifetime something considerably less than twenty thousand dollars.

1980: New Jersey

September 1973:
What I Did Last Summer

What I did last summer. I did many things last summer. I wrote three novels in the Berkley *Lone Wolf* series. I did some short stories. I did a novelization of the Lindsay Anderson film *O Lucky Man!* but it's never going to be published, unfortunately, because Lindsay Anderson wants to do his *own* version with stills from the picture. Boy was I mad! Not as mad as Warner Books, though, who are out twenty-five hundred dollars. I'm not giving it back, Jack. Those are some of the things I did last summer. I went to Saratoga with my family and lost three hundred dollars. I got a new Calais Coupe and drove it all over Bergen and Rockland counties looking for a way out. (No luck.) But the important and memorable thing I did last summer was to write a science fiction novel.

It is called *Tactics of Conquest* and Pyramid Books will publish it in January. I have already seen it in galleys; it is what they call a rush job. A copy editor called me last week to check a certain term and to ask if I had ever heard of Bobby Fischer, adding, "By the way this is a very good novel, not at all like science fiction." Was it exciting to hear that! But of course it is *just* like science fiction. I wrote it in four days for a four thousand dollar advance. It is fifty-five thousand words.

Here is how I got to write the novel: an editor named Roger Elwood got a contract with Pyramid Books to deliver twelve science fiction novels and he called on me to do one. Whew! Before I had even said yes he handed me a contract and it called for two thousand dollars right then. I didn't even have to offer any material. Or a plot outline or synopsis or anything. Just sign the contracts in June promising to deliver the novel by August 1 because Roger Elwood needed to deliver his first book fast. I was proud. Two thousand dollars for signing your name makes you proud. But then I knew that I had to write a whole novel in less than a month by the time the two thousand dollars came into my hands and I got scared. I never write anything until the money gets into my hands. That is the smart and shrewd way to deal when you are mostly working in paperback original.

It sure is scary writing a novel on a one-month deadline. But I knew what to do. Even though it is only six and a half years since my first sale to *Galaxy* I am an experienced science fiction writer with a lot of novels to my credit and the first thing you need is to write a novel fast, particularly in science fiction where you can't fill up the pages with fornication like in the other stuff, is to have something to base it *on*. It is always easier to rework something already written. For one thing it reminds you that you got the thing done once somehow and can do it again, and for another it gives you something to hang on to.

So I decided to expand a twenty-six-hundred-word short story I had written last November called "Closed Sicilian" which I sold to *Fantasy and Science Fiction* for eighty dollars. It was a chess story describing a fool's mate in four moves from the point of view of the fool, who is so arrogant that he doesn't know what has happened to him, even at the end. I based the story on the world chess championship matches during the summer of 1972 in Reykjavik, Iceland. Bobby Fischer, who beat poor Boris Spassky, struck me as being an interesting character for a short story narrator since he had no insight at the same time that he was megalomaniacal. Also I had spent all this time staring at the television where they got the moves in from Iceland one by one and had experts talking about them. I had to do something to justify all of that staring, right? Because science fiction is the only thing I know how to sell (other than mysteries and pornography and novelizations that Lindsay Anderson won't let go through), I framed it as a science fiction story, so I had my narrator and opponent playing for the fate of the universe with the aliens as referees. I have done this kind of thing before and dealing with aliens controlling the fate of the universe gave me a warm, comfortable feeling as I sat down at the typewriter on Tuesday afternoon, August 2 or 3 it must have been. "What are you going to do now?" a neighbor had asked me a few minutes before while I was standing outside looking at the trees as if for the last time. "I'm going to write a novel in four days," I said. "You don't mean that," the neighbor said and giggled. I could tell that she thought I was crazy but that didn't bother me. Everyone here where I live who has heard that I am a science fiction writer thinks that I am crazy, except those who think I am really a criminal or dirty movie distributor. After all, none of them have ever seen my books. I mentioned the story length.

Now you may think that you would have trouble expanding a twenty-six-hundred-word story into a fifty-five-thousand-word novel. You would be right. My oh my did I pad and overload! Sentences became pages, paragraphs became chapters. Megalomania became grandiosity with lots of examples. Whole flashback chapters were devoted to his life as a chess champion: scenes in Berne and Moscow and Philadelphia, the traveling life of the chess master. Also some sex scenes, but within good taste because this is the science fiction market. It turns out that the narrator has really had a secret homosexual relationship with his opponent for years but it is said in a subtle way.

Roger Elwood, when I delivered the novel, wanted the narrator and his opponent to be the same person but I said nothing doing. I have my integrity. I did write the epilogue he wanted, though, where the world gets destroyed. For four thousand dollars you don't get sticky. It is the biggest advance I ever got in my life.

I wrote the novel in four days filling in all of the background and details that the short story implied. I smoked many cigarettes—I know this is bad and I'll cut down soon—and drank ten ounces of scotch a day, five before lunch and five before dinner. Also beer. It helped me not to vomit when I ate and did I eat! When I finished the novel, it was late Friday; I said to myself, you've worked four days and made four thousand dollars. That is smart. That is good. Who makes a thousand dollars a day in Bergen County? Not even shrinks or crime bosses make a thousand a day. At least, not consistently.

I was so proud. I had shown the world what a fine writer I was and Roger Elwood and Pyramid Books how quick. I knew they would appreciate it. I mailed the novel to Roger and he called me and said he liked it so much he would like me to do *another* Pyramid novel. So now I am thinking of what I can do. I think I will expand my story "A Galaxy Called Rome," which I also wrote last summer. I can fill in on that too, and this story is nine thousand words, not twenty-six hundred, which makes it easier to bloat. Roger only wants to pay me thirty-five hundred dollars for this one though because *Tactics of Conquest* and the new program at Pyramid have to prove themselves in the market. I think I'll take it. That is still almost nine hundred dollars a day and who in Bergen County is making nine hundred dollars a day? I am smart and shrewd and doing better than almost any thirty-four-year-old in Bergen County. That is what I did last summer and what I will do this fall, and *next* summer too until I make so much money that I can stop doing all of this and really enjoy my life. I know that I will enjoy my life once I can relax but first I have to do this "Galaxy Called Rome" thing, and then I will get back to the *Lone Wolf* stuff. I am going to end this composition now because I am very tired and you only asked for fourteen hundred words on what I did last summer and here they are and I hope my fourteen-dollar check will be payable on receipt because I really need the money. I really do. I always will. I'll make sure of it.

1980: New Jersey

The Cutting Edge

Everyone plays with ten-best lists; science fictioneers are no exception,* but here is a modest proposal: the ten best science fiction stories of all time. Whether it is possible to define a ten (or even a hundred) "best" is arguable; the qualifications and criteria of the compiler are pressed every step of the way but that the job should be done for the short story too is *non disputandum.*

Science fiction, at the cutting edge, has always flourished in the short story. Perhaps the genre by definition will sustain its best work in that form; here a speculative premise and a protagonist upon whose life that premise is brought to bear can be dramatically fused with intensity. Novels tend to be episodic or bloated; even novellas tend to say too much or too little, but the short story—traditionally defined as a work of prose fiction of less than fifteen thousand words—has from the outset comprised as a body most of the best work in this field. While science fiction in its modern inception has produced possibly ten novels that might be called masterpieces, it has given no less than several hundred short stories that would justify that difficult and presumptuous label. Henry James defined the short story as in its purest state being about one person and one thing and it is within that compass that science fiction achieves rigor and its proper form. (It should be noted that almost all of the disputed masterpieces that would appear on most of the ten-best-novel lists were ex-

---

* I have a best novel list footnoted elsewhere, and Harlan Ellison dared to name the ten best living writers in the field in a book review column for *Fantasy and Science Fiction* in May 1974. In fact, Ellison who could never be accused of backing off a big fight to find a little one, *ranked* the writers.

panded or assembled from short stories . . . Budrys's *Rogue Moon*, Miller's *Canticle for Leibowitz*, Sturgeon's *More Than Human*, for instance. Although one is dangerously surmising author intention, it would be a fair guess that these were originally conceived as short stories and only worked *obiter dicta* into novels, lending further justification to the view of science fiction as a short story form.)

Too, it is in America in the twentieth century that the short story has reached its apotheosis; our one great contribution to world culture might be the American short story, which has become a wondrous and sophisticated medium. The confluence of the American short story and that uniquely American form modern science fiction would result in a ten-best list with which anyone would reckon.

Herewith this list with the usual qualifications and cautions: The stories themselves are not ranked in order of descending merit (it is foolish enough to find a top ten without going on to arrange them); the judgement is based upon literary excellence (seminal stories such as Stanley Weinbaum's "A Martian Odyssey" as influences upon the genre have had far greater effect than most of the stories on this list, but the work is being judged *sui generis*) and, of course, as a single informed opinion it is liable to provoke challenge and dispute, not least of all from the list-maker himself, who a year or two from now might want to change three quarters of it . . . or ten years from now might agree that work yet to be written has displaced several of these stories. Whether or not our *best* work is ahead of us, a lot of good work is still ahead:

1) "Vintage Season," by C. L. Moore (*Astounding Science Fiction*, 1946). Published as by "Lawrence O'Donnell," the second most important (after "Lewis Padgett") of the Kuttners' pseudonyms, this story is now known to have been one of the very few of their eighteen-year marriage and collaboration to have been written by Catherine Moore alone. The vision of future cultural decadence imposed (through time-traveling researchers who specialize in attending plagues,

torment and disasters of history) upon an earlier (undefined) period that in its own decadence *foreshadows* this version of the future, its languorous pace, concealed but artful, and manipulated erotic subtext and stylistic control probably distinguish it as the single best short story to emerge from the decade. It has been rewritten endlessly and has directly influenced hundreds of short stories and at least two dozen novels, but none of its descendants have improved upon the basic text. Its only flaw—as Damon Knight pointed out twenty years ago—is a denouement that carries on too long between the revelation and the flat, deadly last line; it is bathetic and overextended and for the sake of good form should have been severely cut. It is not a serious flaw because it enables the reader only to marvel at the spareness of this eighteen-thousand-word story to that point; it has the density and emotional impact of a novel.

2) "Her Smoke Rose Up Forever," by James Tiptree, Jr. (Alice Sheldon) (*Final Stage*, 1974). The judge must plead his own problem at the outset and throw himself on the mercy of a higher court: I commissioned this story for an original anthology coedited with Edward L. Ferman and published it first. *Final Stage* was a written-to-order anthology in which various writers were asked to write a story on one of the great themes of science fiction, Tiptree (Sheldon) was asked for an End of the World story and delivered one of the very few masterpieces that did not originate with the writer. (Editorial involvement or the assignment of theme often results in good stories and sometimes improves good stories to better-than-good, but masterpieces almost necessarily have to self-generate and will themselves through.)

This postapocalypse story in which the end of the world becomes a metaphor for the shocks and injuries of existence which prefigure and replicate death (and make the state of death their eternal reenactment) is almost unknown today; it appears only in the out-of-print *Final Stage* in hardcover and paperback and an out-of-print Tiptree collection, *Star Songs of an Old Primate*. It will reward the most careful study, and Tiptree's afterword to the story—also commissioned, as were all of the afterwords in the collection—is a brief but beautifully written essay on the real meaning of science fiction on whose ideas I have based the title essay of this book.

3) "Particle Theory," by Edward Bryant (*Analog*, 1977). The protagonist, a physicist, is dying of cancer, his emotional life is in decay and the astronomical phenomena which he observes clearly foreshadow the end of the world . . . all three levels of destruction here fuse, echo one another, are bound together in a story of astonishing excellence which fully meets the criteria of a great science fiction story: its science and scientific premise are locked into the text and grant the emotional force; without the scientific element the story would collapse, yet it is this speculation's shift into individual pain and consequence which clarify it scientifically. The seventies were science fiction's richest decade in the short story; although more good stories were published in the fifties, the top 1 or 2 percent of the latter decade's output far exceeded the equivalent top percent of the fifties, and in this decade Bryant's story might have been the best.

4) "The Terminal Beach," by J. G. Ballard (*New Worlds*, 1965). Rejected by every American market of its time as eventless, internalized and depressing, this mysterious and beautiful work was the key story of its decade, the pivot for science fiction; its importance lay not only in its depiction of "inner space," the complex and tormented vistas of the human spirit in the post-technological age, but in its use of science fiction technique to convert its ambiguous landscape, and by implication our century, to "science fiction."

5) "Private Eye," by Henry Kuttner and C. L. Moore (*Astounding Science Fiction*, 1949). A puzzle story, a futuristic

mystery (how can the protagonist make a premeditated murder look accidental when the forensic pathologists and the prosecution have time-scanning devices that can follow him from birth and put him on stage all the time?) that in its horrid denouement indicates exactly where the Kuttners thought the paraphernalia and technological wonders of the future would take us and why; cleanly written, paced to within an inch of its life and although still anthologized, it is nonetheless always underrated as the masterpiece that it is.

6) "Sundance," by Robert Silverberg (*Fantasy and Science Fiction*, 1969). A complex, multiply voiced, shifting point of view (employing among other technical devices, second-person narration for a time), the story would have been self-conscious, a display of virtuosity for its own sake, were it not for the pain of the American Indian protagonist attached to a genocidal mission and the clarity of its plot development, which not only justify but incorporate all of the stylistic trickeries and make them implicit in the theme. It is the most brilliant of many Silverberg excellences in the short story form between 1968 and 1975, and in its subtle fashion is one of the most powerful anti-Vietnam, antiwar stories of the period.

7) "Anachron," by Damon Knight (*Worlds of If*, 1954). A story which, because it did not sell the top magazines of the period, fell into obscurity, although it does appear in the recent *The Best of Damon Knight*. A time paradox story of the most elegant construction it sets up and explodes its desperate conclusion with a remorselessness and rigor characteristic of the very best of the *Galaxy* school of science fiction, of which Knight in turn was the best and most rigorous example. Naturally Horace Gold rejected it, but "Anachron" was only one of many distinguished stories published by James Quinn in *Worlds of If*. Quinn was an editor who—by the standards of science fiction perhaps rather foolishly—asked first that a story be literate and readable and only sec-

ond that it be suited for the nebulous "science fiction audience."

8) "The Men Who Murdered Mohammed," by Alfred Bester (*Fantasy and Science Fiction*, 1954). Bester is best known for his two fifties novels which appeared first in *Galaxy*, *The Demolished Man* (1952) and *The Stars My Destination* (1956), but in that period he published no more than a dozen stories in *Fantasy and Science Fiction* which are generally thought to be the finest and most consistently brilliant body of shorter work by any writer in the history of the form; here is Bester using the device of the time paradox to destroy the time paradox and some of the shibboleths of science fiction itself (*"you* are your past . . . each of us lives alone and returns alone"); the many-voiced, restless, surgically probing style is beyond the level of the best "literary" writers of Bester's time. (It was the late nineteen-sixties before the so-called mainstream in the persons of Robert Coover, a latter-day Norman Mailer, Donald Barthelme, Robert Stone caught up to Bester by finally evolving a style which crystallized the fragmented, tormented, transected voices of the age.)

9) "Fondly Fahrenheit," by Alfred Bester (*Fantasy and Science Fiction*, 1954). Silverberg has called this perhaps the single finest short story ever to come from science fiction; it may be. It certainly is, with due respect to "Sundance" (which was written a full decade and a half later!), the most technically brilliant: an alternating first and third person, a maddened protagonist and the crazed robot who has become his alter ego and *doppelganger*, perfect demented control and a trapdoor ending. There has been nothing like this story in modern American literature; that it was published over a quarter of a century ago and is still unknown outside of science fiction is an indictment of the academic-literary nexus, which in the very long run, if there is any future for scholarship at all, will pay heavily.

10) "E for Effort," by T. L. Sherred (*Astounding Science Fiction*, 1947). A. J. Budrys writes that Campbell published Sherred's first story on its astonishing merit, spent the next ten years thinking about it and decided that he didn't like what it really meant at all. A viewer which enables its possessor to see anyone at any time in history, once seized (as it would inevitably be) by the government, will be so obviously dangerous to all other governments that war will be started as soon as the word gets out; technology in its purest form will always be appropriated for the purposes of destruction. Sherred has published only a scattering of short stories and a forgotten novel (*Alien Island*, 1968) over succeeding decades; his reputation on the basis of this story remains as secure as that of any writer in the history of the genre.

The second ten, all close runners up to be sure, are listed again in no order and with the understanding that any or all could be traded in for any or all of the top ten:

"Baby Is Three," by Theodore Sturgeon (*Galaxy*, 1952); "Live at Berchtesgarden," by George Alec Effinger (*Orbit*, 1970); "They Don't Make Life Like They Used To," by Alfred Bester (*Fantasy and Science Fiction*, 1961); "The Ninth Symphony of Ludwig van Beethoven and Other Lost Songs," by Carter Scholz (*Universe*, 1977); "The Eve of the Last Apollo," by Carter Scholz (*Orbit*, 1977); "The Psychologist Who Wouldn't Do Awful Things to Rats," by James Tiptree, Jr. (*New Dimensions*, 1976); "The Children's Hour," by Henry Kuttner and C. L. Moore (*Astounding*, 1944); "Timetipping," by Jack M. Dann (*Epoch*, 1975); "The Big Flash," by Norman Spinrad (*Orbit*, 1969); and "Party of the Two Parts," by William Tenn (Philip Klass) (*Galaxy*, 1955).

1980: New Jersey

Son of the True and Terrible

There is no way in which a contemporary audience—even the contemporary audience for "serious" fiction—can understand the degree of humiliation and self-revulsion many science fiction writers suffered until at least the mid-nineteen-sixties. Philip K. Dick in a recent introduction to his collection *The Golden Man*, has written movingly of this; all through his first decade it was impossible for a science fiction writer to be regarded by writers in other fields or in the universities as a writer at all. College professors of English regarded the genre as subliterate; the timeless man on the street thought it crazy. Word rates were low, the readership was limited and one operated from the outset with the conviction that work of even modest ambition would live and die within the same room that the debased did. Dick remembers meeting Herbert Gold at a party in the fifties and asking for his autograph; Gold gave him a card inscribed "to my colleague, Philip K. Dick," and Dick carried this around for *years*. It was the first acknowledgement from a person of literature that his work existed.

Philip Klass has an even grimmer anecdote in his essay "Jazz Then, Musicology Now" published in a 1972 *Fantasy and Science Fiction* "college issue." (At that time courses on science fiction at the universities were in the first flush; a little innocent capitalization never sent any of us to jail. Nor should it.) In 1945, Klass and a graduate student in English of his acquaintance met Theodore Sturgeon in an automat; Sturgeon (whose "Killdozer!" had just about then been published in *Astounding*) talked passionately and at length of the artistic problems of science fiction, the particular challenges of the genre and the demands of a medium in which expository matter was of central importance to a story yet could not be permitted to overbalance it. After Sturgeon left them, Klass's friend said with an amused laugh, "These science fiction writers, they really think of themselves as writers, don't they? I mean he's talking about this stuff seriously as if he were writing literature!"

A writer who came into this field after 1965 cannot really know what it must have been like for Sturgeon and Dick, Kornbluth and Sheckley. At no time has it ever been easy to attempt serious work in this form, but after 1965 science fiction's audience had increased: there was some crossover of that audience and the audiences for literature of other sorts, and because of Sputnik, the assassinations, the Apollo Project and the employment of the clichés of the form by certain successful commercial novelists—Drury, Wallace, Levin all had bestsellers which were thematic science fiction—the form had a certain grudging cachet; people might not know what you were writing (or care about it) but at least they had *heard* of it. In the nineteen-fifties the only people other than crazy kids who would even admit to knowledge of the form were a few engineering or scientific types and they kept the magazines well hidden.

There must have been a lot of rage in these fifties writers, rage and recrimination and (most commonly) self-loathing for even being involved in the form and, after a while (because you fell into the habits and also because you became labeled), being unable to write anything else unless one was willing to repudiate the totality of one's career, adopt a pseudonym and start all over again. That rage was fueled by low advances, capricious editors, predatory publishers, policies in the book markets which consigned any science fiction novel to a defined audience, printed or overprinted a given number of copies and after throwing them into the market out-of-printed the book (and then cheated on the royalty statements). It was fueled yet further by the perception that most of these writers had of the disparity between their work—galaxies, world-conquering, heroes, superheroes, galactic drives, the hounds of heaven—and their lives, which were limited, entrapped, penurious and often drenched with alcohol. Even a moderately intelligent writer could see the disjunction and its irony; some dealt with it by writing witty and highly ironic science fiction, but others went deeper into megalomania and fantasy and their promise was lost. And none of these writers were helped by the fact that television and the movies were appropriating their work to make cheap, mass-market pap of it; sometimes they paid low rights fees (Campbell got five hundred dollars for the movie rights to "Who Goes There?"), but most often they simply plagiarized. The fifties science fiction writer was a true van Vogt protagonist: surrounded by vast, inimical, malevolent powers who regarded him without compassion, struggling to reach some kind of goal which he could not define. But unlike the Gosseyns the fifties science fiction writer had no weapon shops of Isher, no Korzybskian logic, no seesaw, no secret plans, no occasionally helpful Overlords. He had only his colleagues to help him along and they were in as much trouble as he. Under these circumstances, the body of work turned out by the twenty or thirty best is a monument to the human spirit (or its perversity) unparalleled in the history of the so-called arts.

"What you have to do with this stuff," a science fiction editor said a long time ago, "is to sit down with the outline and crank it; reel it out like porn. Otherwise it doesn't pay, if you really get involved with it, try to have original conceptions or at least work them out originally you'll slow down and can't make any money. If you're going to write science fiction for a living or even as part of a living you have to do it fast."

Without evaluating these remarks (they are true for most of us; even in the decade of five-figure advances the average return for a science fiction novel in all its editions is still about five thousand dollars), they function as partial explanation as to why no science fiction writer has published more than two or three books of the first rank.

In 1960, in fact, reviewing A. J. Budrys's *Rogue Moon*, James Blish stated that no science fiction writer had ever written more than *one* masterpiece (he concluded his review by suggesting that if Budrys were able to come back to the field and get work done he might be the first to break the pattern), and even two decades later there is not much evidence in contradiction; Silverberg has done five or six novels which are very strong, and so has Philip K. Dick, but even now as we regard the Le Guins or Delanys or Wolfes, even James Blish himself (who was a strong writer), who can be said to have published more than two?

The economics of this business may change. Other exigencies will not. Science fiction is a difficult, rigorous, exhausting form demanding at the top the concentration and precision of the chess master and the skills of the first-rate *litterateur*. How often do these qualities intersect in any of us? How often can they be reproduced?

Fortunately, for most, science fiction on the scene-by-scene level can be cranked, can fill space, can be mechanically conceived and rapidly written . . . it *is* a genre, it does have recourse to devices and a handy stock of the familiar. But here too the schism at the center is manifest: there has never been a science fiction novel so bad that breathing in its center was not an idea which once had merit; there has never been one so good that it could not be seen at the bottom to be based upon the clichés and clutter of the form.

No, there ain't nothing so good that we cannot get a glimpse of the worst, ain't nothing so bad that it doesn't demonstrate a little of the good . . . there's the best in the worst of us, worst in the best, all of us dummies of varying workmanship and attractiveness in the service of the Great Ventriloquist who do, he surely do, give voice to us all.

1980: New Jersey

The All-Time, Prime-Time,
Take-Me-to-Your-Leader
Science Fiction Plot

Earlier I offer the continuing dialogue a number of plots or
conceptions which would be—at least from my perspective,
and perspective I have—unsaleable. Truthful as this material
is, it is anything but helpful; if there is any audience for this
book (in truth, there is no other) it is one comprised of
aspirant writers and I would not want them to regard science
fiction as an endless series of Thou Shalt Nots.

Science fiction, to the contrary, represents perhaps the last
open and relatively accessible market in America (if one can
write to format one can still, although just barely, sell without personal acquaintance) and needs all the new material
that it can acquire; the old writers are beginning to perish (if
not mortally at least productively) by the scores now and the
middle-agers like myself are retreating to despair, editing
books of ruminant essays, or continuations of the Albderan
Raiders on the Moon series.

Accordingly and generously I would like to contribute to
the gene pool a number of plots, all of which, granted that
you are a writer of routine proficiency, fluency and dedication
(a drinking acquaintance with the editors in all cases would
not hurt), almost certainly *will* sell. Why shouldn't they?
They have been good enough for the markets for decades;
they should be good until at least the millennium. Perhaps
even the *next* millennium. *Too much of a good thing is not
nearly enough* is the motto of science fiction; *we want more
of what we've got* could be in Latin on the seal of Science

Fiction University, good old Ess Eff You, weak major sports but good javelin and outstanding in track, water polo and wrestling. The aspirant writers are welcome to them in full measure and I seek neither thanks, praise, blame, a share of the advance or a collaboration credit—only honor.

"The Underground": Henry Walker Smith is a youth in the future, let us make it 2312 and be done; this particular extrapolation is based upon some mad extension of present-day circumstance that has overtaken the society.

Okay, let's get *some* use out of the things and use automobiles. In 2312 in Henry's world (it is America but let us be futuristic and call it, say, "Occidentalia") automobiles are banned. The ownership of an automobile, driving it, even concealing knowledge of anyone who owns or drives are criminal offenses. Citizens move around Occidentalia via tramways, chutes, corridors and the like. Most live and work within the same Domicile and only the elite are in need of far conveyance, which is fast jet. Henry has little to do with the elite, accepting his position as a subclerk in the Bureau of Fabrication and Design with the feeling that it is all he could deserve, and to travel more than a very few kilometers from Domicile would be self-indulgent.

We know that Henry is agoraphobic and terrified and can write some amusing scenes in which he reveals this tendency while justifying it to himself as "loving Domicile." That will be one of the key phrases of the book—"loving Domicile"—and perhaps will catch the eye of the fans who will make it part of their lore.

Henry is twenty-three. He enjoys his culture and aspires to be nothing other than a Senior Overclerk in Fabrication & Design, but shortly after the story opens, of course, in Chapter Two, things begin to rapidly change. He falls in because his girlfriend's father is a crook (Marge confesses this tearfully to him the night that he tells her he would like to Co-Domicile) who works with a rowdy bunch keeping forbidden automobiles on a private estate dozens of kilometers from

Domicile. "That's horrible," Henry says as the full implication bursts upon him, "something has to be done for his own sake, I'll turn him in to the Overlords."

"You can't," Marge says, "I love him and besides if you turn him in the Driverists will know exactly who did it and will run you over in a corridor with one of their miniatures." She caresses him soothingly. "Besides," she adds, "cars aren't that bad, they're kind of *fun*. In the old days before Daddy got seedy and turned into a Narcotics Degenerate he used to take all of us out to the estate for drives and let us crash things and watch the great races and it was kind of fun." Her eyes twinkle madly. "You might like it yourself, Henry, not that I'm asking you of course."

"I'd *hate* it," Henry says, "are you saying that part of our Co-Domicile is the condition that I become a Felon? I won't do it," and he decides that he must look at Marge in a new light. Perhaps she is not quite the woman with whom he wants to Co-Domicile. He is awfully young to get into a permanent arrangement anyway, although the Overlords encourage early pair-bonding for their own sinister reasons.

It is, however, too late for Henry; Marge's father, a bumbling but fearful sort, has kept an eye on her relationship and comes to know almost immediately that she has told him about his double life. Before he can go to Headquarters and report the situation, Henry is abducted by the rowdies, spirited from Domicile and taken to their crude and automobile-ringed estate far from there. His struggles during the abduction scene are quickly subdued, his protests are met with laughter, his pleas that he will be thrown out of Fabrication & Design are met with contempt. "Please forgive me, Henry," a tear-streaked Marge says to him when he recovers consciousness (they have finally had to Overnarcotic him so valiantly did he protest) on the estate, "I didn't think that they would do this to you but they're desperate men. Anyway, why don't you just listen to them and try to learn about the situation? You may find that you *like* automobiles. I know that I did."

Henry shakes his head, bitterly retreats to silence, resolves that he will have nothing further to do with her. He may be enchained by desperadoes but he does not have to lose his integrity even though Marge appears every evening after her own shift in Reconstruction & Reminiscence to plead with him to be reasonable. He finally begins to change his attitude when Marge tells him that her father has been imprisoned by the Overlords for circulating a Pro-Automobile petition in a tramway and is now being beaten by them daily. "That's a little excessive," Henry says, breaking his silence, "I mean, they're not even giving an old man a *hearing*. And besides, those cars outside that I can see through the bars are kind of attractive; they glisten in the sun, which is much brighter here than back in Domicile. They said it was all poisoned here but it isn't. Hey, if they lied to us about that one thing they could lie about a *lot* of things? Am I right? Marge, do I have a point there? not that I'm ready to question the authorities to the point of defying them. At least not yet."

"But someday, Henry, you *will*," Marge says, and the first (and last) scene of gentle sexual foreplay is written as Henry and Marge make love Oldstyle (but the scene terminates long before do their thrashings and moanings).

A new and chastened Henry is then educated by the rowdies—who all turn out to have degrees in Traffic Control & Reconstruction; they have been falsely portrayed as ruffians when actually they are scientists whose search for personal freedoms as transmuted into their love for autmobiles have become threatening to the Overlords—into the realities of the situation. What he comes to realize is that in the name of "energy survival" and "cleaning up the environment" the Overlords have managed to erode virtually all personal freedoms. The first encroachments via restriction of automobiles were seen in the last third of the twentieth century; hundreds of years later the Overlords' control is virtually complete except that the scientists have managed to set up the underground kilometers from Domicile and with the use of the retrieved, sacred, reconstructed automobiles are ready to mass an attack upon the oppressors. They need, however, someone who knows everything about the Department of Fabrication & Design for it is deep in that department that the machinery which controls is hidden, and would Henry like to help them?

"I don't know," Henry says, and he is truly uncertain until word reaches them that Marge has been abducted by Overlords who have gotten wind of the situation and are torturing her for information. "I can't save her," her father says, "but I'm going to *try*, by Cadillac I will. I did this to my only daughter and I'll die to get her back."

Looking at the old man Henry hears the thunder of his own heart. "You won't go alone, old man," he says, "I'm going to go *with* you. They lied to us from the beginning but now we know the truth. Don't we?" The scientists nod. "Now we know the truth," Henry says.

He takes driving lessons—there are some comic scenes here —on a replicated 1962 Cadillac Calais Coupe in brown with red leather interior and autotronic eye; at length he is at the head of an invading driving corps of the scientists who in seventy automobiles roar through the barriers of Domicile and descend upon Fabrication & Design. Marge's father unfortunately dies in the second wave, being chased by the Overlords' distracting robots, who dazzle him with mirrors and cause him to crash into a retaining wall, impaling himself on the steering hub of a replicated 1955 Chevrolet. Henry barely has time to weep at the spectacle before he is plunged into the sweeping combat scenes of the last chapters; he overcomes the Overlords' defenses, fights his way to the heart of the bureau and confronts the Chief Overlord. "You're dead, Henry Walker Smith," the cowardly Overlord says from behind his shield, but Henry (still in his car) uses the autotronic beam to dazzle the knave and then does away with him by backing the car with its protuberant, deadly tail fins into his belly. The Overlord expires with a gush.

Henry, breathing hard, is barely able to enjoy the triumph before he remembers that Marge is unaccounted for. She falls, however, from behind one of the walls of the Overlord's Chamber in deshabille; she had been tied up for subterranean sexual purposes but, fortunately, not yet ill-used. "You did it, Henry," she says, "now we can Domicile together forever."

"Not so soon," Henry says grimly, holding her, "Marge, not so soon." His face has the look of eagles; a spare and haunting cast. He has matured greatly within these months as who, granted his experiences and insight, would not? "It isn't that easy and it isn't over."

"Oh Henry—"

"We must return to the countryside, find more automobiles and continue the liberation. There are other Domiciles."

"You're magnificent, Henry."

"But at the end of all of it," he says, holding her lightly, "a little peace and the reconstruction of the internal combustion engine, the turbomatic transmission, dual radials with sidebar kit and the luxury package with two-tone strips and soft-ride finish."

Marge kisses him lightly.

"We'll get there," he says.

"Remembering the Old Man": The Old Man, let us call him Lothar, is a beggar on Mule IV in the Vegan system; very old and dirty he lives at the virtual bottom of the corrupt, feudal, technologically oppressive society of the 87th Century Human. "There is a better time for all of us coming," he chants as he pleads for coins and sweetmeats from the occasional tourists who comprise the only element of the economy of this picturesque but poverty-stricken backwater planet. "We have had a great history and our time will come again." The tourists think that he is crazy but harmless; the governmental forces on Mule IV are too sparse and corrupt to pay any attention to Lothar at all. This is a good thing since Lothar is the last representative of a fallen hierarchy which was obliterated before the memory of all presently in power, to say nothing of the tourists who admire the views, pick up their illegal drugs and return to the rockets as quickly as possible.

Lothar finds a baby abandoned in a nest of concrete pilings. He takes pity upon the child, the government tending to make waste products of humanity, as he thinks, and the poor thing's mother being desperate, and takes him into his humble dwelling where he gives him a name and raises him as his own. Corear goes on the streets with him at an early age, showing intelligence by ingeniously adding some tricks to the nuances of begging.

A great bond of affection unites Corear and Lothar and although their surroundings can hardly be said to improve, their relationship is magnificent. When Corear is eighteen, Lothar dies, passing on as his legacy in an extended and touching deathbed scene a coin to he who is as his son. "For you *are* my son and were always of my flesh," he says mysteriously as he expires. This leaves open-ended as is only proper the question of paternity and imparts ambiguity to the novel. Ambiguity is not to be scorned, particularly when it can be managed with a device as simple as this, one which will not need constant further reference or tie up the progression with dull explanation.

The coin invests Corear with vast psychic powers. He can perceive the thoughts of anyone on whom he focuses, traverse thousands of light years by taking a deep breath and concentrating, move planets in their orbits and cause any human being to submit to his desires. He discovers these powers one by one and slowly over a period of many months, trying to ascertain what might be the best use to which they can be put. (He is sure from the outset that he does not want to take advantage of women to obtain sexual favors.) Through this period he lives in obscurity. However when he sees Lothar's memory being sullied on Mule IV—the old man, for reasons he cannot understand, becomes the object of virulent attacks by the government—he decides that he can stand mute no longer. LOTHAR IS ALL EVIL he sees inscribed on public squares; LOTHAR WAS A BAD MAN is the title of a column in the weekly journal in which scurrilous (and untrue) tales of the old man are told. Corear becomes angry.

He uses the magic coin to quickly dethrone the government and achieve power. Having done so he discovers that Lothar was the deposed ruler of Mule IV thrown out of office decades ago because he had discovered that the planet was merely a front for an enormous, intergalactic drug trade. (Drugs were used then to wipe his memory from the minds of his subjects; no one remembered who he was.) His death had, by preordainment by Lothar himself, caused old holograms to stalk the palace waving accusing fingers and hence the repudiatory measures. They came out of guilt. Corear is saddened to learn all of this but at the least he feels that he has redeemed the good name of Lothar. Who in a final revelation—he goes through the palace documents slowly—turns out to be his father who had sired him unthinking in a final night of lust before he was deposed and who had found him in the streets when his mother had come to him nine months later to report that the government had seized her child upon birth and taken him from the Great Creche.

Corear is moved by all of this and wishes that it had been different, wishes too that at least he had been able to share with Lothar a filial love. Still, it is too late, isn't it? He assumes the throne and rules justly and wisely for thirty-seven years using the coin when necessary to get him out of scrapes. He continues to refuse its possibilities for sexual submission, however, and hence never marries. Or has a relationship with a woman. Although from time to time there might have been opportunities.

"Vigilante!": The brawling and lusty crew of *North Carolina Tarheel*, a medium-sized space surveyor, lands upon a subsidiary planet in the Antares Cluster for a shore leave. There they find themselves—the canny Scot, the redheaded naïve kid eager to learn, the shrewd old engineer, Sparks the Communicator, Lila the Mysterious Captain—in the midst of a planetary revolution.

A corrupt system based upon slavery is being attacked by a disorganized group of vigilantes who have driven them to their plantations but have then run out of weaponry, energies and ideas. The vigilantes plead with the Survey Team their first day on the planet to use their technology and wits to help them, and although Lila feels that the crew should be detached, she does not interfere when the others decide to take part in the revolution. "After all," as Sparks says, "we have to take a position sometime as representatives of a decent galaxy."

The bumbling redheaded kid gets into amusing difficulties in constructing the world-wrecker and is captured by the oppressors, but they are otherwise no match for the Team, who bloodlessly unseat them when the Team persuades that resistance would be hopeless against a world-wrecker. The world-wrecker of course turns out to be papier-mâché and the scheme a bluff but too late for the oppressors. The slaves are freed.

Sparks is asked by the grateful freedom-loving slaves to be King but declines in favor of Lila, who he has always known had as her secret wish a planet to rule. She takes charge of matters—calling herself not King but Queen—while the Team fuels up matter-of-factly and prepares for further adventures. The redheaded kid is taken at one point for a renegade oppressor but just in the nick of time his identity is revealed and he is saved; on this note of comic and joyous relief the Team sails away under command of Sparks, who has always wanted to command a Survey Team, and why not? He gets all of the credit and none of the responsibilities.

(Special note: If the regime being overthrown is *anti*slavery and this is cleverly masked it might be possible to get a magazine sale on this. The regime corruptly wants to give the barbarians the freedom for which they are not prepared and so on and so forth. Whether one wants the better distribution but somewhat lower word rates and ephemeral aspect of the magazines is an individual decision to be sure. It would be difficult to get *both*. Keep in mind that foreign sales can be an important proportion of the eventual income on a book, whereas the magazine publishers purchase world serial rights.)

"Come and Get It": Jones is an old, sickly, half-blind Terrestrial Scout; he is about to be pensioned off after this, his final expedition. Congestive heart failure, failing gall bladder. Unluckily—he has never had extreme luck but in the end gets through, he thinks—he is abducted by a fleet battalion of Rigelians seeping through the stars in search of Terrans who might be able to give them information that can be used in the continuing great war. Jones uses his two pieces of wood in confinement to construct a solar generator, no small feat considering that the two weak suns overlooking this Rigelian outpost are dwarf stars in the last moments of their celestial lifetime.

Nonetheless, a lifetime as a hobbyist engineer is converted to use as Jones stupefies the Rigelians during interrogative sessions with threats of apocalypse; he then brings about a simulated solar eclipse which panics them as myth has informed that darkness portends ten thousand years of nightfall. Oh boy. "Help us," the senior Rigelian begs Jones, "I speak in telepathic hookup for all the millions of us when I beg you most sincerely to let the sun shine again. We can't really deal with this. How much of this do you think we can take?"

"You must surrender," Jones says shrewdly, "and turn over all of your treasure, to say nothing of the prisoners you've taken to Earth."

"Absolutely," the panicked Rigelian says, "just get us out of this!" Jones nods and causes the illusory eclipse to dissolve. The Rigelian babbles gratitude and as a gesture of thanks cures Jones' congestive heart failure (he cannot do much with that gall bladder) and installs him as ruler of the Rigelians, who become a subrace of the Rigelian outpost of Empire Earth.

"Amazing Grace": A prophetess appears amidst the superstitious and primitive peoples of a prehistoric Earth and forecasts the wonders to come: Pyramids, Sphinx, television, radar, automobiles, time travel and guns. The primitives, awed, commit her to death by fire shockingly reminiscent of the death of Joan of Arc. In fact it *is* the death of Joan of Arc.

In an epilogue-flashback the prophetess is seen as an ordinary time-traveling citizen of the fourth millennium about to try an amusing experiment. In going to prehistory she knows she flouts canon, and in planning to tell the natives of the future she lurches into Temporal Apostasy, but she is a stubborn lass. In a further epilogue it is disclosed that none of the events described occurred since, of course, her death by fire would render impossible those events which brought her to it, but in a final *final* epilogue the first paragraph of the story is repeated, indicating that Temporal Paradox is nothing to be trifled with by anyone.

"Hold That Tiger": A child in the American midwest of the early twentieth century is escorted by his father through a marvelous circus in which he sees—

A green beast, a three-horned beast, a magician with taloned hands, a spider with golden web, a polar bear who plays cello (but only in the first position) and a camel who plays violin (but without vibrato and shaky intonation; the duets are dreadful). And similar marvels. "This is wonderful, daddy," the child says, "who made it up?"

"You did," the father says, and would say more except that the polar bear cellist puts down his instrument with determination and whisks the child away. The child is terrified but his roistering screams are thought by the sparse audience to be merely part of a Wonder Screaming Child Presentation and he obtains little satisfaction. The polar bear places him in a tent and waits for the camel, who appears carrying both instruments. The two then play (execrably) the third movement of the Brahms Double Concerto in A Major for Violin and Violincello. The carnival attractions mass to listen and the child sees the magician become a marvelous flower, the flower opening to speed him from dream to the reality of his deathbed at the turn of the millennium.

(Please note: If the intent is the young adult market, the child does not awaken on his deathbed but in his father's arms outside the circus. "Would you rather see this stuff or save a few dollars and go right home?" the father asks. "I'd just as soon take you home now but it's up to you. Everything's up to you. You have to be responsible, you're a young adult now."

("I go home, dada. I go home right now. I go home from this rotten place and I never come back again."

("That's a mature and responsible decision. After all, it's all phony anyway."

("I hope so, dada. I really do.")

I cannot *guarantee* a sale on any of these plots. There are no guarantees in our complex, painful and competitive business. On the other hand I have done the best that I can and I assure you that if you use them you are on the right track. I can in fact promise—assuming as always that you have friends among the editors, and every one of you, as Damon Knight once said, had better make them where you can—a swift and sympathetic reading, a concerned and passionate response, a delayed but viable contract and some time beyond that an advance to speed you through the writing of all these novels and all of their sequels through all the eight to twelve to (if you are a saint) twenty-five years of your productive and creative, your artistic and dedicated, your daring and soul-testing writing career.

1979/1980: *New Jersey*

Grandson of the True
and the Terrible

The most important science fiction writer of the forties was probably Theodore Sturgeon. He was not the best nor the most significant nor did he make the most fundamental impression; even as a stylist (the basis of his reputation) he might have fallen behind the Kuttners in top form, but what Sturgeon did was to keep open the possibility for a kind of science fiction that eventually many others came to do.

That possibility was style-oriented, science fiction built upon configuration and mood. No other writer was doing this. Heinlein was certainly the most important figure of the decade, Asimov probably the most imaginative, van Vogt the most characteristic and crazily inventive, the Kuttners the most polished and adroit . . . but all of these writers were replaceable. There were others who were doing what Heinlein was doing if not nearly so well, similarly Asimov. Their style, their approach to science fiction as an extrapolative medium impressing circumstance upon character was expression of Campbell's vision. The Kuttners were better than good but their depth exceeded breadth and *The New Yorker*, for instance, was full of fine writers (some of whom, like John Collier and Robert Coates, had clearly influenced them). Van Vogt was more *sui generis*, but L. Ron Hubbard knew a few things about the paranoid plot.

If any of these writers had been lifted out of the science fiction of the forties, the forties would have been an inestimably poorer decade . . . but the history of modern science fiction, less their own contribution would be essentially the same. Even Heinlein's work, hardly as skillfully, would have been done eventually.

But Sturgeon's contribution was unique. In his use of style, internalization and quirky characterization he was keeping the door open for everything that happened after 1950 when the Gold, Boucher and fifties perspective became the alternative that dominated the field. If Sturgeon had not been around through his decade to hold the flag for this kind of science fiction, had not established that the literature could be style-oriented, it is possible that the fifties perspective would not have developed; the editors and potential audience might have been there but no basis would have existed upon which writers within the field could build.

Science fiction without Sturgeon might have been a science fiction without *Galaxy*, Walter Miller, Jr., Brian Aldiss, Damon Knight, the original anthology market or *Dying Inside*. And other things. Without Heinlein, Asimov, van Vogt, Hubbard or de Camp the medium would have been the poorer, but without Sturgeon it might by the middle of the fifties have played itself out in extrapolative gimmickry and arcana and not have existed at all.

At least it is something to think about, just as it is to think about what might have happened if Campbell had not been persuaded that Theodore Sturgeon wrote science fiction at all. Just as it is to think about what might have been if Sturgeon—who had serious literary ambitions and wanted to publish in the quarterlies and mass magazines—had not failed in his field of first intention and had had to settle for science fiction. Asimov, Heinlein, del Rey never wanted to write anything else. Sturgeon found his text after the fact. What he wrote reflected this. It made the field first attractive and then possible for many of us.

The fiction writer, locked up with the sound of his own voice, the science fiction writer locked up with the sound of his own voice propagating megalomaniacal or solipsistic visions imposed upon his persona, the *full-time* science fiction writer who professionally does little else . . . contrast these visions with the alienation, isolation, anonymity and impotence which constitute the condition of the American writer—

Taking it all on balance it can be well understood why alcoholism, divorce, depression, fragmentation and a rich history of lunacy characterize science fiction writers and why it was Alfred Bester's considered opinion in the early fifties, after meeting the crowd for the first time, that all of them were brilliant and all of them had a screw loose someplace. (Bester, who wrote radio and television scripts at the time, considered himself at least nominally representative of the Outside World.)

But one does not want to prejudice the case. There is another side and another opinion. John W. Campbell, who must have thought about this too in his time, put it this way to one of his writers in the forties: "People who read science fiction are crazy. We all know about that. And science fiction writers are even crazier. But when you talk about science fiction *editors*, well—"

A long Campbellian sigh.

Silence.

1980: New Jersey

Give Me That Old-Time Religion

Science fiction does not—perhaps it cannot—depict the future. What it does, as A. J. Budrys pointed out back in 1969, is to offer sentimentalized versions of the past or brutalized versions of the present transmuted into a template of the familiar. The future cannot by definition be portrayed; it will require a terminology and ethos which do not exist. Perhaps true science fiction, an accurate foreshadowing of the future if such a thing were at all possible, would be incomprehensible. It is important to point out, however, that as futurologists not only our devices but our credentials are miserable.

It is true—a notorious example—that as late as 1967, no science fiction writer had understood that the landing on the moon would be tied into the media and that it would be observed by several hundred million people including that long-distance station-to-station caller, Richard M. Nixon. None of us. The closest any came was Richard Wilson in a short-short story, "Harry Protagonist, Brain-Drainer" in a 1965 issue of *Galaxy* which speculated that the first landing on Mars, witnessed by most of the population of this planet on Intermedia, would expose the astronauts to the hypnotic and mind-shattering powers of the Secret Martians, who would turn the minds of most of us to jelly.

Not such bad thinking for fifteen hundred words, this story, and handled with Wilson's customary lucidity and *élan* (he is a charter member of the science fiction club larger than Hydra and even more filled with bitterness: Underrated Writers, Inc.), but it had very little to do with the conditions that NASA and the networks were jointly evolving, and the question of mass audience was strictly for the subplot, a means of setting up the satiric point. Wilson takes the NASA-CBS I Saw It Coming Award but only by default, and since the award pays only in honor (of which NASA and CBS have offered us little) Wilson will have to be content with his membership in the club and 1969 Nebula for "Mother to the World."

For the rest of us—Heinlein, Asimov, Clarke, Anderson and the sixties visionaries too, the movers and shakers who were attempting to write Street (as opposed to Street & Smith) Science Fiction—no honor whatsoever and no excuse. That a genre built upon visionary format whose claim to public attention through the early decades had been based upon its precognitive value should have utterly failed to glimpse the second or third most significant social event of the decade is—one puts on one's tattered prophet's robes—quite disgraceful.

Pointless to blame the readership. The readership may not be interested in the visionary, the dangerous, the threatening or the difficult, that is true, but their expectations have been formed by what has been given them. Great writers *make* great audiences. The solemn truth is that as NASA and the networks conspired to reduce the most awesome events of the twentieth century to pap between advertisements and other divertissements, most of us were in the boondocks, slaving away on our portions and outlines and our little short stories, trying to figure out what new variation of Eric Frank Russell we could sneak by Campbell, what turn on a 1947 plot by van Vogt out of a 1956 novel by Phil Dick might work this one last time for Fred Pohl's *Galaxy*. While we slogged on through the mud of the sixties, bombs bursting in air, recycling the recyclable for one thousand dollars in front money, the liars and technicians were working ably to convert the holy into garbage and a damned good job they (and we) made of it too. The liars and the technicians put the space program out of business by the mid-seventies. Perhaps it might have been different if we had stayed on the job . . . but then again we all know that science fiction has almost nothing to do with the future so why feel guilty? *I* don't. And "Harry Protagonist, Brain-Drainer" is still around somewhere for proof that we had a handle on it, so there.

No guilt at all. I was just one of the boys.

1980: New Jersey

SF Forever

I have little idea what the science fiction of the eighties will be like—as we live through, it will seem to be very much like the science fiction of the year just before—but I have a pretty good grasp of the somber nineties. Here is how it will be: mass-market science fiction will edge toward fantasy. Fully 75 percent of novels published under the label will be what we would have defined five years ago as fantastic; some of these books will do extraordinarily well and others will not but there will be little to choose qualitatively. The books that will do well simply will have larger print orders and publicity, which may in certain cases go to television or movie theaters. Series books or novels set against a common background will predominate and writers will (with one another's consent and cooperation) use one another's backgrounds freely. Some series will originate with publishers who will farm them out to various writers and pay flat fees, hold the copyrights. "Hard" or technologically rigorous work will occupy the same small corner of the market that "literary" science fiction does now.

"Literary" science fiction and many backlists will be in the hands of the specialty publishers whose present-day precursors will in the nineties be as influential as medium-sized paperback firms are now. The specialty publishers will range from one-person operations not unreminiscent of the Gnome or Shasta of the fifties to large and well-staffed organizations that will be subdivisions of conglomerate divisions; the arm for "serious" literature. These specialty publishers in the aggregate will be responsible for hundreds of books a year—

the major publishers, amongst them, will do only forty or fifty —and sales will range from a few hundred to a few hundred thousand. All of the larger specialties will have experimented with trade and mass-market paperbacks and will now and then do well enough to bring a title to the attention of the majors, who will do a big edition.

The audience for written science fiction—a hard base of half a million with another two or three million who can be brought in for an occasional title—will remain stubbornly, inflexibly unchanged. This constant will be the barrier against which the specialists will time and again collide and which will cause the weaker publishers to fail since the audience will, once again, be unable to expand with expanded titles.

There will be about as much work of quality as always but none of it will come from the mass-market publishers.

The magazines and the science fiction short story will have little role in the market. The few magazines will serialize some mass-market novels and give some new writers a marginal audience for their first attempts. These two or three magazines will all be owned by the same conglomerate, will be under the same editorship and will pay approximately the word rates which prevailed in the nineteen-fifties.

1980: New Jersey

What I Won't Do Next Summer, I Guess

Here are a selection of plot ideas guaranteed unsaleable in the science fiction market of yesterday, today and any variant of tomorrow. Sorry to bring this up again, folks, but the end is nigh and one must have a unity of vision:

An intelligent culture on a far planet is not carbon-based but perhaps silicone- or silver-based. There is no "organic" deterioration after death and therefore these creatures make no distinction between the living and the dead. The dead remain in residence, are fornicated with, talked to, manipulated, used as the subjects of advertisements, given responsibilities (obviously met poorly; they are shiftless) for work, child care and so on.

The dead are obviously less efficient at most of these tasks than the living but they are humored and tolerated as the senile or extremely aged are in our own culture, and because they do not register organic collapse their presence is not actively unpleasant. In fact, it is kind of reassuring. As well as possible the inhabitants of this culture put a good self-denying face on the inadequacies of the dead just as Victorians would cover up for batty, incontinent relatives on their premises.

A group of missionaries from a carbon-based culture land on this planet, survey the situation and are of course horrified. Gently but very firmly they teach the natives the difference between the "dead" and the "living" and the necessity to "bury" and "put away the memory of" the dead.

Slowly their message works its way through the culture and slowly the natives reach an understanding of the difference between "life" and "death."

Needless to say they are filled with spiritual terror when they realize that the dead are quite different from them and that this difference has to do with the extinction of consciousness. The culture in the face of death's apprehension goes mad, becomes dysfunctional, the natives turn upon the missionaries and kill them and then begin to slaughter one another. The only way to control death, they surmise, is to administer it themselves. (If "death" is a conscious, perpetrated condition rather than an unhappy inevitability, it can be manipulated, threatened, offered or denied.) The culture becomes a charnel house; it becomes centered around the rituals and ordeals of murder.

It does not last much longer.

A Messianic figure in an alternate or future civilization is homosexual and preaches that only through conversion to homosexuality can the present human condition change and the time of Revelation and Reconstruction begin.

The reason for this is practical: universal homosexuality will cancel procreation and bring the ongoing generations to a halt, ending humanity within about a century. This Messiah has prophetic conviction and textual justification; he overcomes all of the manifold social resistance and brings about that era which soon enough will bring to fruition all of the prophecies mysteriously locked within the Book of Daniel.

A science fiction editor who hates the field and is incapable of understanding it rejects every promising writer and idea which is presented, preferring to deal with a tight circle of friends who in return for the editor's contracting for debased material, offer kickbacks. The relative success of the line and the kickbacks enable the editor to amass a sufficient amount of money to become a publisher, where he continues his policies successfully until his house sets the standard for all science fiction. He is finally undone by his success: expansion means that he must hire staff editors, the editors merrily interpose themselves between the publisher and the writers and *they* conduct their business exactly as the publisher does, which is to say that they buy from friends and take kickbacks. Unfortunately, several of the manuscripts that slip through are of sufficient originality and technical facility to sell badly. The publisher loses his commanding edge in the market; by the time he fires his staff and seizes control it is too late, his imprint has lost its reliability and predictability for the audience and before he can sell to a conglomerate he goes bankrupt. His third wife takes their remaining assets and leaves him. He contracts boils.

(It is the template which is the problem here. Make the product matter transmitters rather than novels and you might sell this. To a friend. For a consideration.)

1980: New Jersey

Come Fool, Follify

The editor and I were talking about large science fiction conventions. Editors and writers, fans and mistresses who have hated one another, some of them for forty years, come by the thousands and dwell in the same space for three days. Old passions, old griefs; it must be understood that envy and recrimination in science fiction are higher per capita than anywhere except, possibly, the reform wing of the New York Democratic Party. "It doesn't mean anything, though," the editor said calmly, "if these people were really serious, they'd kill each other."

The capsulization of science fiction. In print and behind one another's backs we* will revile, condemn, curse and whisper scurrilities of the most urgent sort: face to face we are mild and reasonable individuals. Old enemies buy one another fresh drinks; new lovers and old whisper confidences in the corners. Publishers of venomous fanzines will ask writers for autographs. As the editor said, if we were serious we would almost certainly kill but the key to science fiction—perhaps for all I know the key to the Ultimate Mystery—is that it is not a serious field at all. In its gnarled little heart it is, in fact, frivolous.

The nature of the form counsels frivolity. Consider the reader's slack-jawed wonder: faster-than-light travel, haunting sea beasts on the Jovian plain, mutiny on the Antares bypass, alternate and mysterious worlds in which dragons can fly and understand Elizabethan English . . . and then it is time for

---

* There is no way around this. One must face the truth at whatever age; to be born a fool is not to be mandated to *stay* a fool: a liberating discovery at forty-one. Anyway, of what use is unimplicated testimony?

dinner, the Chemistry assignment or the subway transfer. Escape reading, you know. If the reader were to really deal with this material on the level apparently offered he would be quite unable to make the changes: how can one carry on even the gestures of one's life if one is rocketing over Jupiter astride a sea beast? One reads science fiction—even at the age of eight one had better read it this way—in contract; just kidding you know. Not to be taken straight. The same fail-safe factor seems to operate within the science fiction reader† as within the American consumer; no one really believes all those ads, you know. One could go quite insane if one accepted the vision of America squeezed through the interstices of automobile, deodorant or cosmetic commercials. Everyone over the age of two (might it be one?) in the United States knows that ads are . . . well, just ads. As science fiction is just science fiction.

Simil, the writer. Four cents a word, maybe five, portions and outlines, magazine rates, editors, special intergalactic issues, put an 8½ × 11 in the machine and let it go. Whoops! and a flight to Mars. Whee! and an invasion of the capitol by the hired assassins of Merm. Whap! and a parallel universe in which time runs contrawise rather than causally. And how much of this can I get done before dinner, and is *New Dimensions* paying on acceptance these days? The first fine exhilaration of youth becomes, with any kind of persistence at all, the routine of middle age; if it did *not*, if one began to dwell in these universes, take the Merm seriously, incur a deep sense of obligation to imbue the imagined circumstance with the consequence that one knows in the real——‡

The effects of writing science fiction in quantity and over a

---

† Robert Lindner, the late psychiatrist, in *The Fifty-Minute Hour* wrote memorably of a young science fiction reader who did *not* appear to have the fail-safe mechanism and it is for this reason alone that the chapter has become famous in science fiction, often referred to, occasionally anthologized. This is what happens to someone who really *believes* this shit is the word to the wise.

‡ Truth in packaging: Several science fiction writers *have* fallen apart and spent time in mental institutions . . . they all come out in pretty good shape, though, and the proportion of admissions in the field is probably less than amongst the general population.

period of time have been amply discussed, the carryover is not insignificant and the damages are evident. One does, as a science fiction writer, tend to hate a little more richly, cleave a little more tightly, recriminate somewhat more sensationally . . . but only up to a point and quickly beyond that lassitude sets in. It is one thing to despise the old colleague who stole your plot idea from a forgotten Ace Double and got it into hardcover; it is another thing to plot against the wretched editor who bought that book and rejected your own while also making love to your ex-mistress and blackening your name around town; it is another to come up against the swine in the hotel bar* and deal with the situation. A handclasp will suffice and a word of cheer; after all, the son of a bitch may be back in the market someday. Your old colleague who is somewhere upstairs drunkenly fornicating with your ex-wife has been doing this kind of thing since 1953 and you are only one of his victims—he's done more to others, and besides if you recall, you did the same thing to him when you swiped that *Worlds of If* short story idea, a really lovely pivot for your own 1964 Pyramid novel. Who knows what he might be saying about *you*? Besides, the old bastard is consultant now for a medium-sized paperback firm and your agent has some portions and outlines on offer; he might even buy them. Then again, he might not. It depends upon who is on his good side in the next month or so and this convention is certainly no time to throw down the gauntlet. Is it? Let's be reasonable now. Besides, a scene would only make the future more difficult; there's no *end* to this, you see, for a lifetime he and you and the editor (at least until the editor is fired) are going to be showing up at these things and a Philadelphia riot would only lead to a coda in Boston, a recapitulation in St. Louis, a scherzo and variations in London two years from now.

Better to take your losses and live with them. You do—one does, after all—have to deal with these people for the dura-

---

* Everyone at a convention is in the hotel bar, usually simultaneously.

tion; they have been around. All of you have been around since 1953; why should anything change now? Or next week?

You take your losses, you stick the editor with the bill, you look for a new mistress or a now unembittered older one. You go through the weekend and you go home, wherever that may be. If you were serious, yes, you might kill the bastards but then again, if *they* were serious, they would kill you, right? Every loss a gain; every action a reaction, the great mid-century vision of the middle class and science fiction is nothing—anyone who ponders this for five minutes will see it clearly—if it is not a middle-class phenomenon.

1980: New Jersey

The Engines of the Night

Science fiction is the only branch of literature whose poorer examples are almost invariably used by critics outside the form to attack all of it. A lousy western is a lousy western, a seriously intentioned novel that falls apart is a disaster . . . but a science fiction novel that fails illuminates the inadequacy of the genre, the hollowness of the fantastic vision, the banality of the sci-fi writer . . . this phenomenon is as old as the American genre itself (in fact for the first quarter century post-Gernsback, outside media would not even *review* science fiction) and as fresh as the latest rotten book.

Not so long ago, a weak and overextended *bildungsroman* by a newer writer was attacked spitefully in a publication called *The Soho Weekly News;* Jonathan Rosenbaum used the first two thirds of the review to vilify and the rest to conclude that sci-fi writers could not deal with contemporary reality because they apotheosized machinery over mortality, stripped humanity in their fiction of dignity and drained it of the capacity to feel. In so saying, Rosenbaum was not only indicating complete ignorance of most of the serious work done in science fiction since the early 1950s but was patently using a novel by a young writer of indifferent reputation (and no particular standing within the field) to vilify the genre.

The unhappy case is typical. Kingsley Amis wrote a quatrain about it once upon a time. In a 1972 book of literary essays, *Rediscoveries*, devoted to the favorite lost novels of writers of reputation, Walker Percy, in cautiously praising Walter Miller's *A Canticle for Leibowitz* (a novel which has never been "lost" to science fiction but which has been continuously in print since its first appearance in 1959), took the most elaborate pains to point out that although the novel had the *trappings* of "pop sci-fi" it had a more serious undercurrent, that elements of mysticism and religious ambivalence verging on apostasy (subjects close to Percy's own artistic sensibility) were handled in a fashion more complex than was usually the case in science fiction . . . and that the novel might actually reward study by serious readers who would otherwise find science fiction of little interest. It was almost as if Percy had to balance off his enthrallment with *Canticle* against a real fear that unrestricted praise, read in the wrong quarters, could threaten his credentials as a "serious" writer. Never has so trembling a testimony been given a novel. (Reminiscent of the eulogy hesitantly offered for the Meanest Man in Town, "well," the minister said after a long, awkward pause, "he never missed a spittoon.") And in a review of my own *Guernica Night* some years back Joyce Carol Oates took pains to make clear that the novel's concerns were, um, spiritual and metaphysical and that its virtues came from it being unlike the science fiction to which she was accustomed.

Science fiction, as I say, stands alone in literature as being forced to judgement by its weaker examples, denied in praise of its best. Outside of literature there are other examples: the question of racial prejudice, for instance, parallels: the member of the minority must "be a good example of his race" and in so doing exhibits virtues which make him "not really like the rest of them at all" and the bad example sets the standard—"they're all like that." Modern music is like this: infrequent performances of it by the major orchestras as part of the subscription program often lead to venomous critical attacks upon the entire specter of the dissonant or atonal (Pierre Boulez might have been pressed off the podium of the New York Philharmonic for programming so much of that crazy modern junk), and contemporary painters, sculptors or avant-garde directors of stage or film know exactly what I mean. Every weak example of the form is there to be used to pillory all of it. "Modern music," "modern art," "modern dance" become as indistinguishable for the in-

furiated critic (and by implication his audience) as does, pity
its shriveled heart, "science fiction."

Is it because the genre is dangerous and threatening, implies a statement and view of the world which is unbearable
for the unaccustomed? Alice Sheldon (James Tiptree, Jr.)
theorizes so in an essay-afterword to her story "Her Smoke
Rose Up Forever" some years ago; postwar science fiction
raised the possibility that our fate was uncontrollable and the
machines were going to blow us out of existence, and the
middle class as represented by the critics fled this insight, *Oh
please, oh please tell us that it is our swimming pools and
martinis and mistresses and angst which make us so unhappy,
not radioactive dust or the mad engines.* After one brief,
terrified look at genre science fiction in the early postwar period, the middle class flung it into furthest darkness and
dived into the swimming pools of O'Hara's or Cheever's sub-
urbs, the forests of Truman Capote or Eudora Welty's night:
they wanted no part of the possibility that technology had
appropriated the sense or the control within their lives. But
still within is that fear of the nihilistic aspect of science
fiction to which they were briefly exposed, a nihilism—which
like that of modern art, modern music, street theater or
mime—suggests that none of the devices of preventative
maintenance (adultery, alcohol, industry, prayer) really matter much at all.

Which means that our worst examples (or even our medi-
ocrities) will be used over and again as a club to beat away
the form; that our best will be ignored and that all of it will
be denied.

Ah but still. Still, oh still. Still Kazin, Broyard, Epstein,
Podhoretz and Howe: grinding away slowly in the center of
all purpose, taking us to the millennium: the engines of the
night.

1980: New Jersey

Con Sordino

I don't know if science fiction was ever the literature of revelation and deliverance they promised us (that is another essay in another time), but the cutting edge of the eighties is action-packed as they say and without a detectable position. Lords and Snow Queens voyage in pursuit of the lost castle, while on the other side of the planet sexes and social roles are surgically implanted; the hotline keeps communications with the universe at a low-key level while the voyagers can stop in Callahan's franchises along the way, swap a few drinks and lies; out there on the further world snake charmers practice a romantic kind of medicine and so on. It is a distance from the drowned landscapes and bombed-out craters of the late sixties, the gleaming machines and obliterated souls; even the Asimovian protagonists of a decade ago had nervous tics and a sullen intimation that matters, despite technological access, were not working terribly well, but the Snow Queen and Valentine have no such problem. Matters still work, sexes can be traded in like wardrobes and time and again the Magic Snake, rising, enacts its will. "The cutting edge of the future is reasonable, not despairing," I wrote about a year ago, but that does not quite make the case either. "The cutting edge of the future is the non-voting electorate," might have been a little better or like one of those voters swooped upon outside the polls who, even for the sake of television, will make no statement whatsoever. "Secret ballot, chief," these voters say, pushing the equipment aside, "none of your goddamned business. Leave me alone."

Not necessarily without merit. Two decades of opinion

have, after all, led us to the edge of the pit where, blinking, we decided we did not like the contents very much at all; it may indeed be time, as a certain uncommunicative voter told us a while ago, to lower our voices a little. All of us. In the forties, the cutting edge of science fiction indicated that either technology would take over the world or do it in; the fifties had the same opinion of the technicians, the sixties did not, for the most part, want to have much to do with technology altogether* and the seventies reacted to the quarreling voice of history by declaring a pox on all of them. Generalizations all, but consolidation is the key; the eighties of Lords and Queens, Hotlines and Snakes prefer to assume that the argument is settled, the landscape itself being evidence of how it was won, and to deal with the *materiel* itself. "He's published half a million words," someone I know said of a major figure of the late seventies, "and I don't know how he feels about a single thing; I don't know what his position is. This is not good writing or important writing."

I am not sure of this. J. D. Salinger, for instance, has published upward (barely) of half a million words and is a major figure still and might well take the same comment (we know how his *characters* feel but not he); one of the definitions of a certain kind of art might be that it is refractive or expressive, not demonstrative. The more interesting question—or at least the one that I would like to raise in this context—is as to how much the Unvoicing of the eighties might be ascribed to evolution (or devolution) of the genre itself; how much could be said to be imposed from without by sheer editorial or market forces.

Certainly forties science fiction can be seen as a reaction to or against the vision of a single man, John W. Campbell; in the fifties H. L. Gold, Fred Pohl, Anthony Boucher and a few others began to solicit stories and propound a science fiction of satire and of doom, and in the sixties Michael

* *Pace* Niven, Pournelle and all the rest, I am talking about the cutting edge; that which came into the field which was not there before. Replication and reinforcement have always been the staple of any genre.

Moorcock and Harlan Ellison, by pressuring for and pro-
claiming a literature of catastrophe, got a great deal of it. Pon-
derous, detached social forces, the apparent inevitability of
history, can be seen in another context as coming from the
cynical, short-term decisions of a small, powerful cabal; this is
what Emma Rothschild wrote (of the auto industry, subur-
ban sprawl and the death of the cities) in *Paradise Lost*.
Science fiction is an insular field; there has never been a point
in its history in America where one powerfully placed editor
could not, within a short time and for the short term, wreak
change simply through using his power to buy one kind of
story and reject another. The group of editors who have
moved to the center of science fiction publishing in the period beginning in 1975 (science fiction is no longer a magazine field, a point which I trust does not have to be argued
here) have imposed, collectively and individually, their vision
upon science fiction, and the eighties cutting edge may be
sheer reaction. Writers—more now than ever—must go where
the market is or they go nowhere at all.

Who are these editors? Most of them (not all) have little
reading background in science fiction prior to their assumption of their posts, none of them have ever written it. (The
central editors of previous decades were *all* writers or people
who had at least attempted to write in the field.) They have
a scant background in the field and for many of them (again,
not all) science fiction editing is a way station, an apprentice
position on the way to editing something, anything, other
than science fiction. Many regard the field if they regard it at
all as a kind of minor league of American literature; the
players may be trapped on the buses and in unheated locker
rooms, most of them, but the coaches and managers whose
future is not as closely linked to their skills can hope to move
on. One way to move on is to win the pennant of course but
that is risky and often impossible on a low team budget; a
more assured way is not to make trouble.

Not to make trouble. Conglomeratization, the fact that
these editors work for minor implements of publishing com-

panies which are in themselves merely minor, if highly visible, parts of the conglomerates is a point that has been made often and by others than myself; the conglomeratization of publishing has had and will probably continue to have a numbing effect upon most work that does not fit neatly into the balance sheet, "literary" work, that is to say, or work of political or social controversy. But it is less a question here of censorship than of self-censorship; given only a marginal understanding of science fiction and only a superficial grasp of its history (to most contemporary science fiction editors "modern" science fiction began with Harlan Ellison, and they have only the most superficial acquaintance with the work of the forties, fifties and even nineteen-sixties), these editors tend to publish what looks like science fiction and their view is necessarily parochial and, granted the nature of conglomeratization, not without fear. "Most science fiction editors seem mostly to seek the assurance that they are doing nothing wrong," Samuel R. Delany writes in *The Jewel-Hinged Jaw: Notes on the Language of Science Fiction*, "and since I cannot grant them this assurance I stay away from most of them."

The nature of professionalism is adaptation and there is no gainsaying that a clever and talented writer can produce work of consequence even under the greatest of strictures. (One need only to reflect for a moment upon the career of Gogol or Günter Grass.) Still it is all very wearying and energy that might be expended in other directions is simply to be applied more lucratively in the detail work; Castles and Queens and Hotlines can be depicted lovingly; snakes (outside of the Book of Genesis) are not political. One must go where the market is; in previous decades it was possible for a certain kind of science fiction writer to create a market but science fiction was then something of an outlaw. Now it is a minor subdivision of Pillage & Homogenize, Inc., presided over in almost all cases by the same group of people.

One could find all of this reasonably discouraging and perhaps I do but Queens and Castles are reaching an audience much larger than all of the work of the previous thirty years *in toto* and audiences are not contemptible to any of us; never were. That all of the Queens and Castles reek of fantasy, that the lines between science fiction and fantasy are being rapidly obliterated and that the cutting edge is moving away from science fiction as it evolved for half a century is more distressing, but that is the topic for another screed in a different time; it is the fibrillating heart of science fiction itself to which I would like to administer CPR had I but the wit, the cunning and the cool refusal to panic.

1981: New Jersey

Corridors

Ruthven used to have plans. Big plans: turn the category around, arrest the decline of science fiction into stereotype and cant, open up the category to new vistas and so on. So forth. Now, however, he is at fifty-four merely trying to hold on; he takes this retraction of ambition, understanding of his condition as the only significant change in his inner life over two decades. The rest of it—inner and outer too—has been replication, disaster, pain, recrimination, self-pity and the like: Ruthven thinks of these old partners of the law firm of his life as brothers. At least, thanks to Replication & Disaster, he has a brief for the game. He knows what he is and what has to be done, and most of the time he can sleep through the night, unlike that period during his forties when 4 A.M. more often than not would see him awake and drinking whiskey, staring at his out-of-print editions in many languages.

The series has helped. Ruthven has at last achieved a modicum of fame in science fiction and for the first time—he would not have believed this ever possible—some financial security. Based originally upon a short novel written for *Astounding* in late 1963, which he padded for quick paperback the next year, *The Sorcerer* has proven the capstone of his career. Five or six novels written subsequently at low advances for the same firm went nowhere but: the editor was fired, the firm collapsed, releasing all rights, the editor got divorced, married a subsidiary rights director, got a consultant job with her firm, divorced her, went to a major paperback house as science fiction chief and through a continuing series of coincidences known to those who (unlike Ruthven) always seemed to come out a little ahead commissioned three new Sorcerers from Ruthven on fast deadline to build up cachet with the salesmen. They all had hung out at the Hydra Club together, anyway. Contracts were signed, the first of the three new Sorcerers (written, all of them in ten weeks) sold 150,000 copies, the second was picked up as an alternate by a demented Literary Guild and the third was leased to hardcover. Ruthven's new, high-priced agent negotiated a contract for five more Sorcerers for $100,000.

Within the recent half decade, Ruthven has at last made money from science fiction. One of the novels was a Hugo finalist, another was filmed. He has been twice final balloted for a *Gandalf*. Some of his older novels have been reprinted. Ruthven is now one of the ten most successful science fiction writers: he paid taxes on $79,000 last year. In his first two decades in this field, writing frantically and passing through a succession of dead-end jobs, Ruthven did not make $79,000.

It would be easier for him, he thinks, if he could take his success seriously or at least obtain some peace, but of this he has none. Part of it has to do with his recent insight that he is merely hanging on, that the ultimate outcome of ultimate struggle for any writer in America not hopelessly self-deluded is to hang on; another part has to do with what Ruthven likes to think of as the accumulated damages and injuries sustained by the writing of seventy-three novels. Like a fighter long gone from the ring, the forgotten left hooks taken under the lights in all of the quick-money bouts have caught up with him and stunned his brain. Ruthven hears the music of combat as he never did when it was going on. He has lost the contents of most of these books and even some of their titles but the pain lingers. This is self-dramatization, of course, and Ruthven has enough ironic distance to know it. No writer was ever killed by a book.

Nonetheless, he hears the music, feels the dull knives in his kidneys and occipital regions at night; Ruthven also knows that he has done nothing of worth in a long time. The Sorcerer is a fraud; he is far below the aspirations and intent of his earlier work, no matter how flawed that was. Most of these new books have been written reflexively under the purposeful influence of scotch and none of them possesses real quality. Even literacy. He has never been interested in these books. Ruthven is too far beyond self-delusion to think that the decline of his artistic gifts, the collapse of his promise, means anything *either*. Nothing means anything except holding on as he now knows. Nonetheless, he *used* to feel that the quality of work made some difference. Didn't he? Like the old damages of the forgotten books he feels the pain at odd hours.

He is not disgraced, of this he is fairly sure, but he is disappointed. If he had known that it would end this way, perhaps he would not have expended quite so much on those earlier books. The Sorcerer might have had a little more energy; at least he could have put some color in the backgrounds.

Ruthven is married to Sandra, his first and only wife. The marriage has lasted through thirty-one years and two daughters, one divorced, one divorced and remarried, both far from his home in the Southeast. At times Ruthven considers his marriage with astonishment: he does not quite know how he has been able to stay married so long granted the damages of his career, the distractions, the deadening, the slow and terrible resentment which has built within him over almost three decades of commercial writing. At other times, however, he feels that his marriage is the only aspect of his life (aside from science fiction itself) which has a unifying consistency. And only death will end it.

He accepts that now. Ruthven is aware of the lives of all his colleagues: the divorces, multiple marriages, disastrous affairs, two- and three-timing, bed-hopping at conventions; the few continuing marriages seem to be cover or mausoleum . . . but after considering his few alternatives Ruthven has nonetheless stayed married and the more active outrage of the earlier decades has receded. It all comes back to his insight: nothing matters. Hang on. If nothing makes any difference then it is easier to stay with Sandra by far. Also,

she has a position of her own; it cannot have been marriage
to a science fiction writer which enticed her when they met
so long ago. She has taken that and its outcome with moder-
ate good cheer and has given him less trouble, he supposes,
than she might. He has not shoved the adulteries and recrimination in her face but surely she knows of them; she is not
stupid. And she is now married to $79,000 a year, which is
not inconsiderable. At least this is all Ruthven's way of ra-
tionalizing the fact that he has had (he knows now) so much
less from this marriage than he might have, the fact that
being a writer has done irreparable damage to both of them.
And the children. He dwells on this less than previously. His
marriage, Ruthven thinks, is like science fiction writing itself:
if there was a time to get out that time is past and now he
would be worse off anywhere else. Who would read him?
Where would he sell? What else could he do?

Unlike many of his colleagues, Ruthven had never had ambitions outside the field. Most of them had had literary pretensions, at least had wanted to reach wider audiences, but
Ruthven had never wanted anything else. To reproduce, first
for his own pleasure and then for money, the stories of the
forties *Astounding* which moved him seemed to be a sensible
ambition. Later of course he did get serious about the category, wanting to make it anew and etc. . . . but that was
later. Much later. It seemed a noble thing in the fifties to
want to be a science fiction writer and his career has given
him all that he could have hoped for at fourteen. Or twenty-
four.

He has seen what their larger hopes have done to so many
of his peers who started out with him in the fifties, men of
large gifts who in many cases had been blocked in every way
in their attempts to leave science fiction, some becoming
quite embittered, even dying for grief or spite, others accepting their condition at last only at the cost of self-hatred.
Ruthven knows their despair, their self-loathing. The effects
of his own seventy-three novels have set in, and of course
there was a time when he took science fiction almost as

seriously as the most serious . . . but that was *later*, he keeps
on reminding himself, *after* breaking in, after publication in
the better magazines, after dealing with the audience directly
and learning (as he should have always known) that they
were mostly a bunch of kids. His problems had come later
but his colleagues, so many of them, had been ambitious
from the start, which made matters more difficult for them.

But then, of course, others had come in without any
designs at all and had stayed that way. And they too—those
who were still checking into *Analog* or the Westercon—were
just as miserable and filled with self-hatred as the ambitious,
or as Ruthven himself had been a few years back. So perhaps
it was the medium of science fiction itself that did this to
you. He is not sure.

He thinks about things like this still . . . the manner in
which the field seems to break down almost all of its writers.
At one time he had started a book about this, called it *The
Lies of Science Fiction*, and in that bad period around his
fiftieth birthday had done three or four chapters, but he was
more than enough of a professional to know that he could
not sell it, was more than ready to put it away when *The Sorcerer* was revived. That had been a bad time to be sure; ten
thousand words on *The Lies of Science Fiction* had been his
output for almost two full years. If it had not been for a little
residual income on his novels, a few anthology sales, the
free-lance work he had picked up at the correspondence
school and Sandra's occasional substitute teaching, things
might have bottomed. At that it was a near thing, and his
daughters' lives, although they were already out of the house,
gave Sandra anguish.

Ruthven still shudders, thinking of the images of flight
which overcame him, images so palpable that often they
would put him in his old Ford Galaxie, which he would drive
sometimes almost a hundred miles to the state border before
taking the U-turn and heading back. He had, after all, absolutely nowhere to go. He did not think that anyone who had
ever known him except Sandra would put him up for more

than two nights (Felicia and Carole lived with men in odd arrangements), and he had never lived alone in his life. His parents were dead.

Now, however, things are better. He is able to produce a steady two thousand words a day almost without alcohol, his drinking is now a ritualized half a pint of scotch before dinner and there are rumors of a larger movie deal pending if the purchaser of the first movie can be bought off a clause stupidly left in his contract giving him series rights. Ruthven will be guest of honor at the Cincinnati convention three years hence if the committee putting together the bid is successful. That would be a nice crown to his career at fifty-seven, he thinks, and if there is some bitterness in this—Ruthven is hardly self-deluded—there is satisfaction as well. He has survived three decades as a writer in this country, and a science fiction writer at that, and when he thinks of his colleagues and the condition of so many with whom he started he can find at least a little self-respect. He is writing badly, *The Sorcerer* is hackwork, but he *is* still producing and making pretty big money and (the litany with which he gets up in the morning and goes to bed at night) nothing matters. Nothing matters at all. Survival is the coin of the realm. Time is a river with banks.

Now and then, usually during the late afternoon naps which are his custom (to pass the time quicker before the drinking, which is the center of his day), Ruthven is assaulted by old possibilities, old ambitions, old dread, visions of what he wanted to be and what science fiction did to him, but these are, as he reminds himself when he takes his first heavy one at five, only characteristic of middle age. Everyone feels this way. Architects shake with regret, doctors flee the reservation, men's hearts could break with desire and the mockery of circumstance. What has happened is not symptomatic of science fiction but of his age, his country. His condition. Ruthven tells that to himself, and on six ounces of scotch he is convinced, *convinced* that it is so, but as Sandra comes into the room to tell him that dinner is seven minutes away he thinks that someday he will have to get *The Lies of Science Fiction* out of his desk and look at it again. Maybe there was something in these pages beyond climacteric. Maybe he had better reconsider.

But for now the smells of roast fill the house, he must drink quickly to get down the half-pint in seven minutes, the fumes of scotch fill his breath, the scents and sounds of home fill all of the corridors and no introspection is worth it. None of it is worth the trouble. Because, Ruthven tells himself for the thirty-second time that day (although it is not he who is doing the counting) that nothing nothing nothing nothing nothing matters.

Back in the period of his depression when he was attempting to write *The Lies of Science Fiction* but mostly trying to space out his days around alcohol, enraged (and unanswerable) letters to his publishers about his out-of-print books and drives in his bald-tired Galaxie . . . back in that gray period as he drove furiously from supermarket to the state border to the liquor store, Ruthven surmised that he had hit upon some of the central deceptions which had wrecked him and reduced him and so many of his colleagues to this condition. To surmise was not to conquer, of course; he was as helpless as ever but there was a dim liberation in seeing how he had been lied to, and he felt that at least he could take one thing from the terrible years through which he had come: he was free of self-delusion.

Ruthven thought often of the decay of his colleagues, of the psychic and emotional fraying which seemed to set in between their fifth and fifteenth years of professional writing and reduced their personal lives and minds to rubble. Most were drunks, many lived in chaos, all of them in their work and persona seemed to show distress close to panic. One did not have to meet them at the conventions or hang out with them at the SFWA parties in New York to see that these were people whose lives were askew; the work showed it. Those who were not simply reconstructing or revising their old stories were working in new areas in which the old control had gone, the characters were merely filters for events or possessed of a central obsession, the plots lacked motivation or causality and seemed to deal with an ever more elaborate and less comprehended technology. Whether the ideas were old or new, they were half-baked, the novels were padded with irrelevant events and syntax, characters internalized purposelessly, false leads were pursued for thousands of words. The decay seemed to cut across all of the writers and their work; those that had been good seemed to suffer no less than the mediocre or worse, and there was hardly a science fiction writer of experience who was not—at least to Ruthven's antennae—displaying signs of mental illness.

That decay, Ruthven came to think, had to do with the very nature of the genre: the megalomaniacal, expansive visions being generated by writers who increasingly saw the disparity between Spaceways and their own hopeless condition. While the characters flourished and the science gleamed the writers themselves were exposed to all of the abuses known to the litterateurs in America and—intelligent, even the dumbest of them, to a fault—they were no longer able to reconcile their personal lives with their vision: the vision became pale or demented. At a particularly bleak time, Ruthven even came to speculate that science fiction writing was a form of illness which, like syphilis, might swim undetected in the blood for years but would eventually, untreated, strike to kill. The only treatment would be retirement, but most science fiction writers were incapable of writing anything else after a while and the form itself was addictive: it was as if every potential sexual partner carried venereal disease. You could stop fucking but only at enormous psychic or emotional course, and *then* what? Regardless, that virus killed.

Later, as he began to emerge from this, Ruthven felt a little more sanguine about the genre. It might not *necessarily* destroy you to write it if you could find a little personal dignity and, more importantly, satisfactions outside of the field. But the counsel of depression seemed to be the real truth:

science fiction was aberrant and dangerous, seductive but particularly ill-suited to the maladjusted who were drawn to it, and if you stayed with it long enough, the warpage was permanent.

After all, wasn't science fiction for most of its audience an aspect of childhood they would outgrow?

This disparity between megalomania and anonymity had been one of the causes of the decay in his colleagues, he decided. Another was the factor of truncation. Science fiction dealt with the sweep of time and space, the enormity of technological consequence in all eras, but as a practical necessity and for the sake of their editors all science fiction writers had to limit the genre and themselves as they wrote it. *True* science fiction as the intelligent editors knew (and the rest followed the smart ones) would not only be dangerous and threatening, it would be incomprehensible. How could twenty-fourth century life in the Antares system be depicted? How could the readership for an escape genre be led to understand what a black hole would be?

The *writers* could not understand any of this, let alone a young and gullible readership interested in marvels that were to be made accessible. (Malzberg had been into aspects of this in his work but Ruthven felt that the man had missed the point: lurking behind Malzberg's schematics was the conviction that science fiction *should* be able to find a language for its design, but any penny-a-word stable hack for *Amazing* in the fifties knew better and Malzberg would have known better too if he had written science fiction before he went out to smash it.) So twenty-fourth century aliens in the Antares system would speak a colloquial Brooklynese, commanders of the Black Hole Explorer would long for their Ganymede Lady. The terrific would be made manageable, the awesome shaped by the exigencies of pulp fiction into the nearby. The universe would become Brooklyn with remote dangerous sections out in Bushwick or Greenpoint but plenty of familiar stops and safer neighborhoods.

The writers, awash in the market and struggling to live by

their skills, would follow the editors and map out a universe to scale . . . but Ruthven speculated that the knowledge that they had drained their vision, grayed it for the sake of publication, had filled them first with disappointment and finally self-hatred: like Ruthven they had been caught early by the *idea* of science fiction; transcendence and complexity and however far they had gone from there, they still felt at the base that this was a wondrous and expensive genre. Deliberately setting themselves against all for which the field had once stood could not have been easy for them. Rationalization would take the form of self-abuse: drink, divorce, obesity, sadism, in extreme cases penury, drugs or the outright cultivation of death. (Only H. Beam Piper had actually pulled the trigger on himself but that made him an honest man and a gun collector.) That was your science fiction writer, then, an ecclesiastic who had been first summoned from the high places and then dumped in the mud of Calvary to cast lots with the soldiers. All for a small advance.

That had been some of Ruthven's thinking, but then he had been very depressed. He had done a lot of reading and thinking about the male mid-life crisis. Sandra and he were barely dealing with one another; they lived within the form of marriage but not its substance (didn't everyone long married end that way?). His sexual panic, drinking, terror of death and sense of futility were more characteristic, perhaps, of the climacteric than of science fiction. The poor old field had taken a lot of blame over its lifetime (a lifetime, incidentally, exactly as long as Ruthven's: he had been born on April 12, 1926) for matters not of its own making, and once again was being blamed for pain it had not created. Maybe.

It wasn't science fiction alone which had put him in the ditch at late mid-life, Ruthven thought, any more than science fiction had been responsible for Hiroshima, Sputnik, the collapse of Apollo or the rotten movies of the nineteen-fifties which had first enticed and then driven the public away. The field had been innocent witness to much of these and the target of some but it was unfair to blame the genre for what seemed (at least according to the books he read) an inevitability in middle class, middle aged, male America.

It was this ambivalence—the inability to fuse his more recondite perspective with the visceral, hateful feeling that science fiction had destroyed all of their lives—which stopped *The Lies of Science Fiction*. Ruthven does not kid himself: even if the contracts for *The Sorcerer* had not come in and his career turned around, he probably would have walked away from the book. Its unsaleability was a problem but he knew that he might have sold it *somewhere*, an amateur press, and he had enough cachet in the field to place sections here and there in the fan magazines. It wouldn't have been much but it would have been more per diem than what Sandra was making or he from the correspondence school.

But he had not wanted to go on. His commitment, if anything, had been to stop. Ruthven from the modest perspective of almost four years, can now admit that he was afraid to continue. He could not bear to follow it through to the places it might have taken him. At the worst, it might have demonstrated that his life, that all of their lives in science fiction, had been as the title said: a lie . . . a lie which would lead to nothing but its replications by younger writers, who in turn would learn the truth. The book might have done more than that: it could have made his personal life impossible. Under no circumstance would he have been able to write that book and live with Sandra . . . but the drives on the Interstate had made it coldly evident that he had nowhere else to go. If he were not a middle-aged, married science fiction writer, then what was he?

Oh, it was a good thing that *The Sorcerer* had come through and that he had gotten back to fiction. The novels were rotten but that was no problem: he didn't *want* to be good any more, he just wanted to survive. Now and then Ruthven still drives the Interstate in his new Impala; now and then he is still driven from sleep to stare at the foreign editions . . . but he no longer stares in anguish or drives in fury; everything seems to have bottomed out. Science fiction can still do many things to him but it no longer has the capacity to deliver exquisite pain, and for this he is grateful.

Eventually someone else, perhaps one of the younger writers, *will* do *The Lies of Science Fiction* or something similar, but of this in his heart is Henry Martin Ruthven convinced: he will never read it. He may be dead. If not he will stay clear. Science fiction now is only that means by which he is trying to hang on in the pointless universe and that which asks that he make anything more of it (what is there to make of it?) will have to check the next bar because Henry Martin Ruthven is finished. He knows the lies of science fiction, all right. But above all and just in time, he knows the truths of it too.

Ruthven attends the Cincinnati World Convention as guest of honor. At a party the first night in the aseptic and terrifying hotel he is surrounded by fans and committee, editors and colleagues, and it occurs to him that most of the people in these crowded rooms were not born when he sold his first story, "The Hawker," to *Worlds of If* on August 18, 1952. This realization fills him with terror: it is one thing to apprehend in isolation how long he has been around in this field and how far the field in its mad branching and expansion has gone from all of them who started in the fifties, but it is quite another to be confronted in terms that he cannot evade. Because his career has turned around in the decade, most of these people have a good knowledge of his work, he is guest of honor, he is hardly ignored, but still—

Here and there in the packed three-room suite he sees people he knows, editors and writers and fans with whom he has been at conventions for years, but he cannot break out of his curious sense of isolation and his conversations are distracted. Gossip about the business, congratulations on having survived to be a guest of honor, that sort of thing. Ruthven would almost prefer to be alone in his room or drinking quietly at the bar but that is obviously impossible. How can a guest of honor be alone on the first night of his convention?

It would be, among other things, a commentary on science fiction itself and no one, least of all he, wants to face it.

None of his family are here. Felicia is no surprise: she is starting her second year of law school in Virginia and could not possibly miss the important early classes; besides, they have had no relationship for years. Maybe never. Carole had said that she might be in from Oakland, would do what she could, but he has heard that kind of thing from Carole before and does not expect her. The second marriage is falling apart, he knows, Sandra will tell him that much, and Carole is hanging on desperately (he surmises) much as Ruthven himself hung on years ago when, however bad it might be, there was nothing else. He wishes that he could share this with Carole but of course it would be the finish of him. There are hundreds of sentences which said to the wrong people would end his marriage on the spot and that is another of them.

Sandra did want to be here but she is not. She has been feeling weak all year and now at last they have a diagnosis: she will have a hysterectomy soon. Knowing what being guest of honor meant to him Sandra had offered to go regardless, stay in the room if she could not socialize, but Ruthven had told her not to. He knew that she did not want to come, was afraid of the crowds and the hysteric pulse and was for the first time in her life truly afraid of dying. She is an innocent. She considers her own death only when she feels very ill.

Not so many years ago, being alone at a large convention, let alone as guest of honor, would have inflamed Ruthven. He would have manipulated his life desperately to get even a night away alone, a Labor Day weekend would have been redemption . . . but now he feels depressed. He can take no pleasure from the situation and how it occurred. He is afraid for Sandra and misses her a little too, wishes that his daughters, who have never understood him or his work, could have seen him just this once celebrated. But he is alone and he is beginning to feel that it is simply too late for adultery. He has had his opportunities now and then, made his luck, but well past fifty and into what he thinks of as leveling out,

Ruthven has become resigned to feeling that what he should have done can be done no more—take the losses, the time is gone. There are women of all ages, appearance and potential here, many are alone, others in casual attachments, many—even more than he might imagine he suspects—available. But he will probably sleep alone all the nights of this convention, either sleep alone or end up standing in the hotel bar past four with old friends drinking and remembering the fifties. The desperation and necessity are gone: Sandra is not much, he accepts this, but she has given him all of which she is capable, which makes her flaws in this marriage less serious than Ruthven's because he could have given more. His failure comes from the decision, consciously, to deny. Perhaps it was the science fiction that shut him down. He just does not know.

Ruthven stands in the center of the large welcoming party, sipping scotch and conversing. He feels detached from the situation and from his own condition; he feels that if he were to close his eyes other voices would overwhelm him . . . the voices of all the other conventions. Increasingly he finds that he has more to hear from—and more to say to—the dead than to the living. Now with his eyes closed, rocking, it is as if Mark Clifton, Edmond Hamilton, Kuttner and Kornbluth are standing by him glasses in hand, looking at one another in commiseration and silence. There is really no need for any of them to speak. For a while none of them do.

Finally, Ruthven says as he has before, "It hurts, doesn't it? It hurts." Kuttner nods, Kornbluth raises a sardonic eyebrow. Mark Clifton shrugs. "It hurts," Clifton says, "oh it hurts all right, Henry. Look at the record." There seems nothing more to say. A woman in red who looks vaguely like Felicia touches his arm. Her eyes are solemn and intense. She has always wanted to meet him, she says; she loves his work. She tells Ruthven her name and that she is a high school English teacher in Boston.

"Thank you," he says, "I'm glad you like the books." Everybody nods. Hamilton smiles. "You might as well," Kornbluth says with a shrug, I can't any more and there's really nothing else." Ruthven shrugs. He tells the woman that the next scotch is on him or more properly the committee. He walks her over to the bar. Her hand is in his. Quickly, oh so quickly, her hand is in his.

At eight-fifteen the next evening Ruthven delivers his guest-of-honor speech. There are about three thousand in the large auditorium; convention attendance is just over ten thousand but 30 percent is not bad. Most attendees of modern world conventions are not serious readers now; they are movie fans or television fans or looking for a good time. Ruthven has thought for months about this speech and has worked on it painfully.

Once he thought—this was, of course, years ago—that if he were ever guest of honor at a major convention he would deliver a speech denunciatory of science fiction and what it did to its writers. Later, when he began to feel as implicated as anyone, the speech became less an attack than an elegy for the power and mystery that had been drained by bad writing and editing, debased by a juvenile audience. But after *The Lies of Science Fiction* had been put away and the edge of terror blunted, the very idea of the speech seemed childish. He was never going to be guest of honor and if he were, what right did he have to tell anyone anything? Science fiction was a private circumstance, individually perceived.

Nonetheless he had, when the time came to plan, considered the speech at length. What he decided to do, finally, was review his career in nostalgic terms, dropping in just enough humor to distract the audience from the thrust of his intention because after bringing his career up to date he wanted to share with them his conviction that it did not matter. Nothing mattered except that it had kept him around until the coincidence of *The Sorcerer*, and *The Sorcerer* meant nothing except that Ruthven would not worry about money until he was dead. "Can't you see the overwhelming futility of it?" he would ask. "The Lies of Science Fiction" seemed a good title except that it would be printed in the convention book and be taken as a slap at the committee and indeed the very field which was doing him honor. Better to memorialize his book through the speech itself. Anyway, the title would have alerted the audience to the bitterness of his conclusion. He wanted to spring it on them.

So he had called it "Me and the Cosmos and Science Fiction," harmless enough, and Ruthven delivers the first thirty-two minutes of his thirty-five minute address from the text and pretty much as he had imagined. Laughter is frequent; his anecdotes of Campbell, Gold and Roger Elwood are much appreciated. There is applause when he speaks of the small triumph of the science fiction writer the day Apollo landed. "We did that," he remembers telling a friend, "at three cents a word." The audience applauds. They probably understand. This much, anyway.

Then, to his astonishment and disgust, Ruthven comes off the text and loses control. He has never hated himself so. Just as he is about to lift his head and explain coldly that none of it matters his voice falters and breaks. It has happened in the terrible arguments with Sandra in the old days and in the dreams with Kornbluth, Hamilton, Kuttner and Clifton, but never before in public, and Ruthven delivers the last paragraphs of his speech in a voice and from a mood he has never before known:

"We tried," he says. "I want you to know that, that even the worst of us, the most debased hack, the one-shot writer, the fifty-book series, all the hundreds and thousands of us who ever wrote a line of this stuff for publication: we tried. We tried desperately to say something because we were the only ones who could, and however halting our language, tuneless the song, it was ours.

"We wanted to celebrate, don't you see? We wanted to celebrate the insistent, circumstantial fact of the spirit itself, that wherever and in whatever form the spirit could yet sing amidst the engines of the night, that the engines could extinguish our lives but never our light, and that in the spaces between we could still thread our colors of substantiation. In childhood nights we felt it, later we lost it, but retrieval was always the goal, to get back there, to make it work, to justify ourselves to ourselves, to give the light against the light. We tried and failed; in a billion words we failed and failed again, but throughout was our prayer and somewhere in its center lived something else, the mystery and power of what might have been flickering.

"In these spaces, in all the partitions, hear our song. Let it be known that while given breath we sang until it drew the very breath from us and extinguished our light forever."

And then, in hopeless and helpless fury, Ruthven pushes aside the microphone and cries.

1980: New Jersey

L'Envoi

MALZBERG, BARRY N. Science fiction writer; references: The Science Fiction Encyclopedia, Contemporary Authors, Bibliography of Modern Science Fiction Writers, Who's Who in the East, 1975–1977 edition. Second violin section, North Jersey Symphony Orchestra since 1976. Vice-Chairman, Program Committee.